Stained Glass
Coloring Book

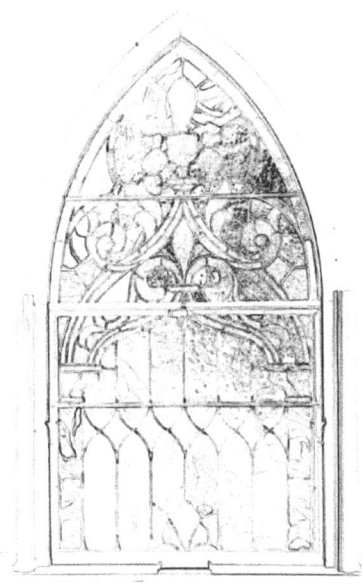

**A portion of all sales will be donated
to local shelters and those in need.**

Another creative product from
www.AuthorRichardETodd.com

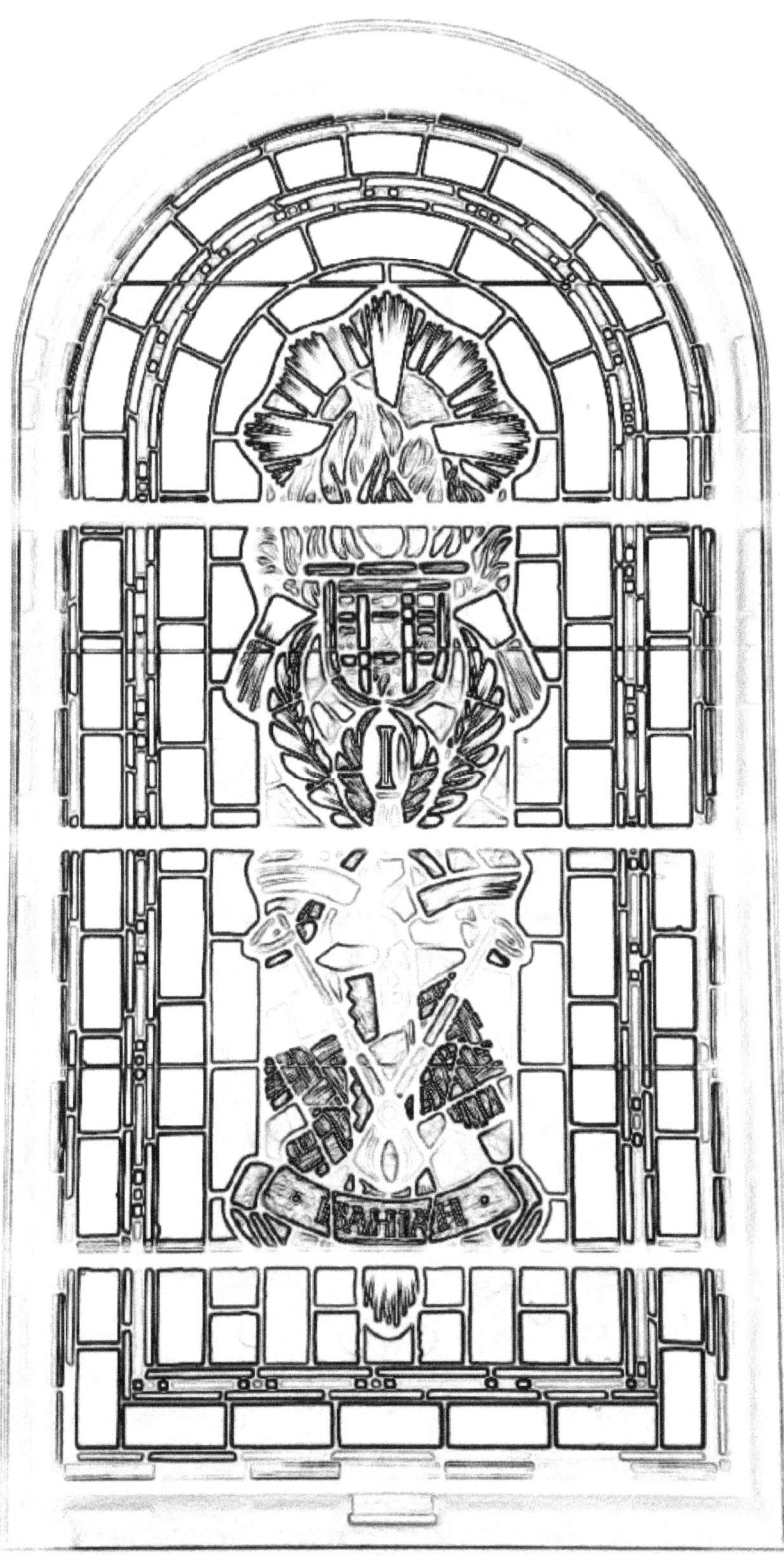

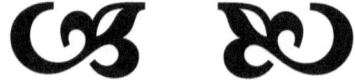

The term **stained glass** can refer to
any colored glass material or work
of art created from it.

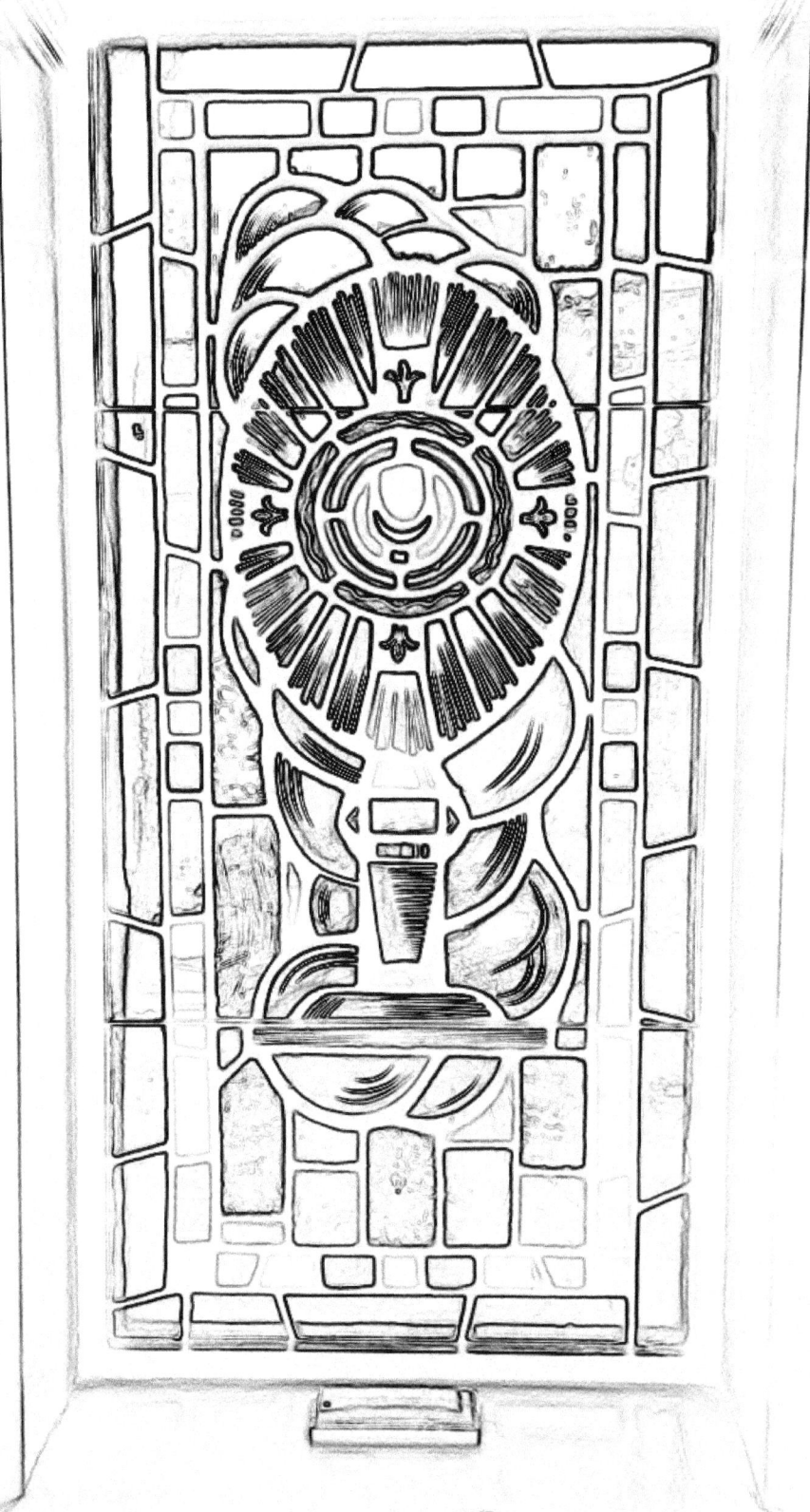

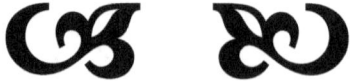

Throughout its thousand-year history, the term **stained glass** has been applied almost exclusively to windows in churches and other major buildings.

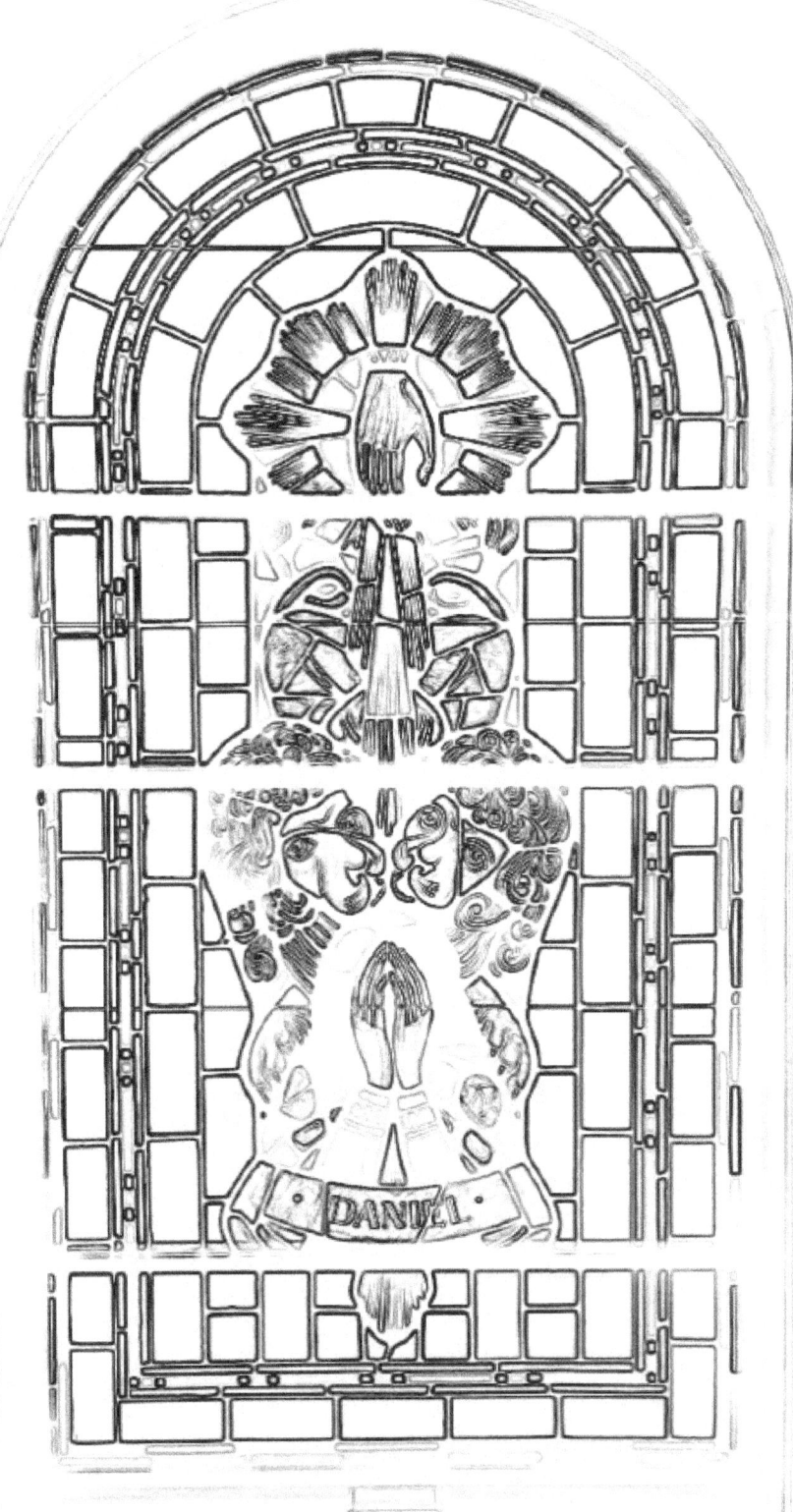

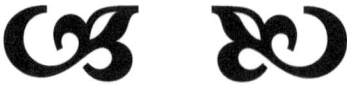

Stained glass is traditionally made in flat panels and used as windows. Modern artists can also create three-dimensional structures and sculptures with stained glass.

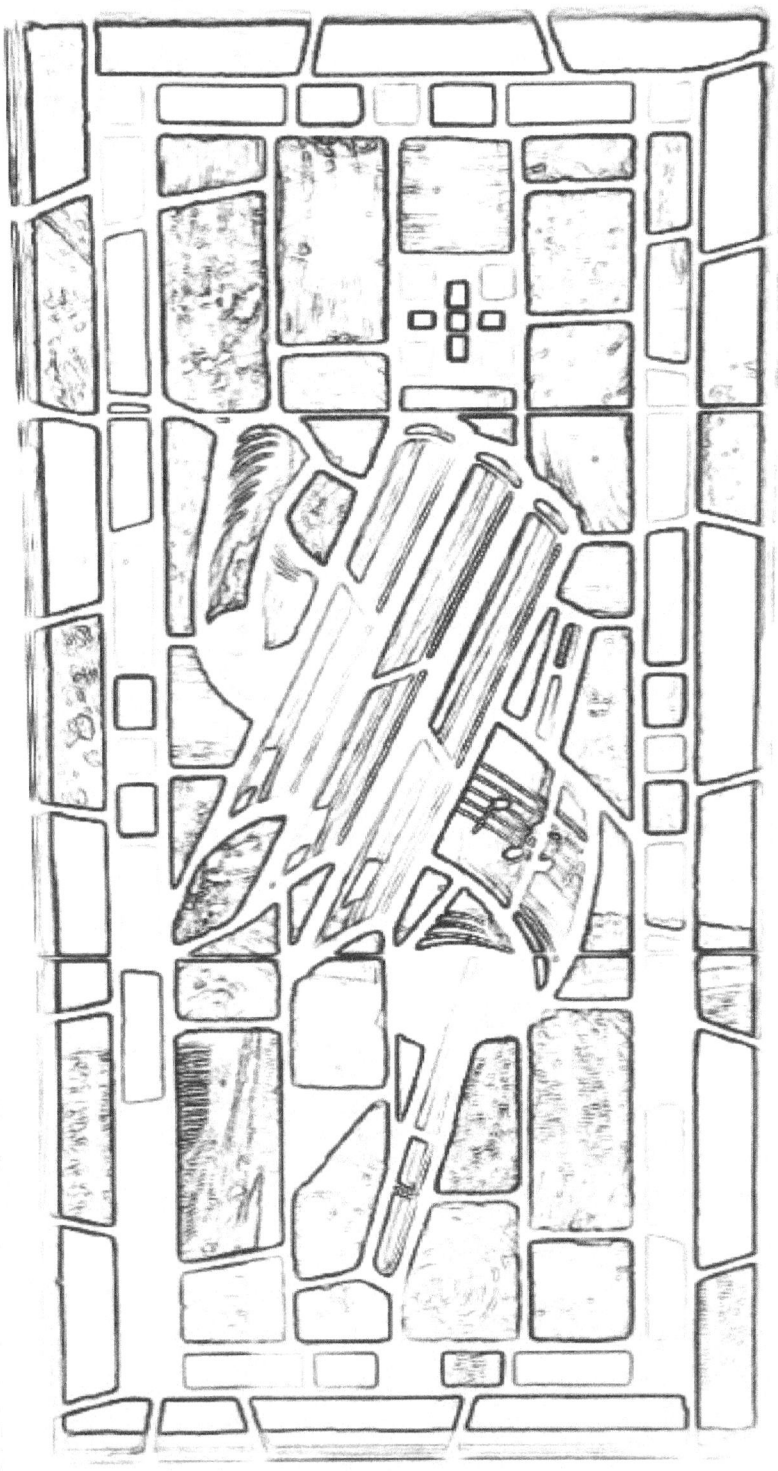

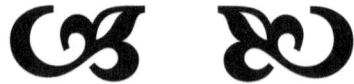

Stained glass is glass that has been colored by adding metallic minerals during the creation process.

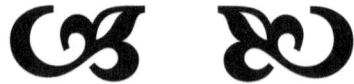

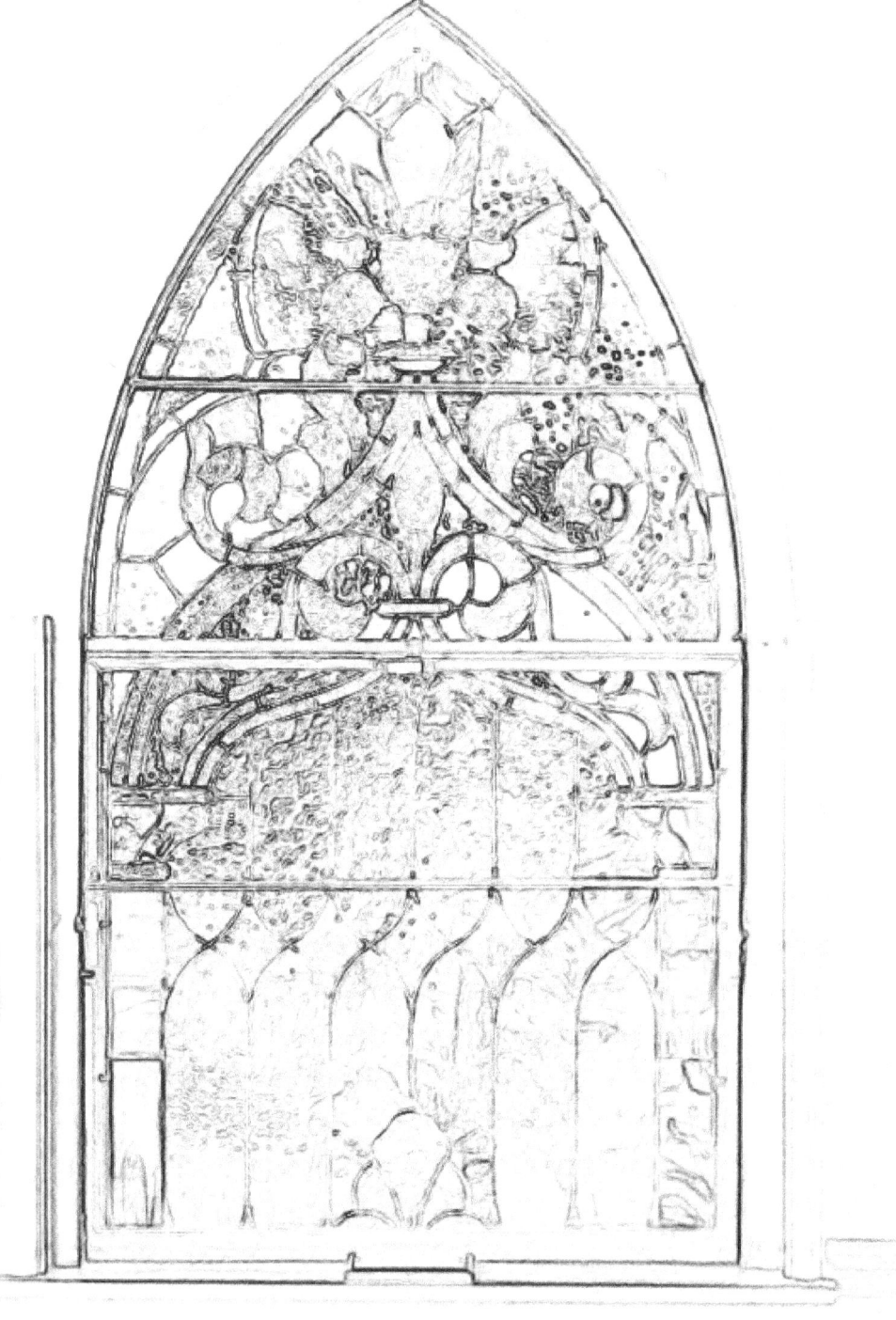

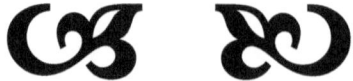

Small, colored pieces of glass are arranged into patters or pictures, held together by lead strips and supported by a rigid frame to create **stained glass** windows.

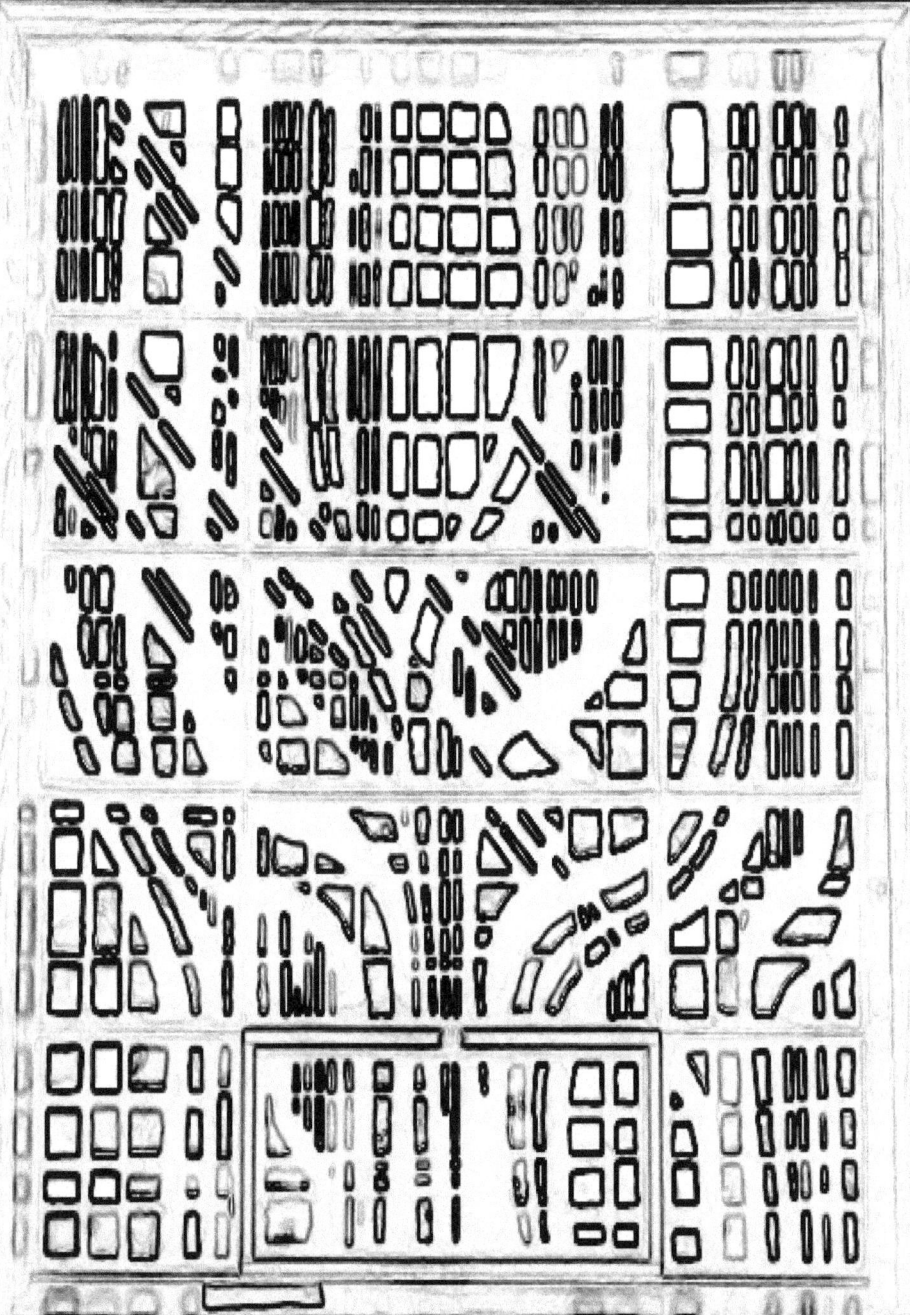

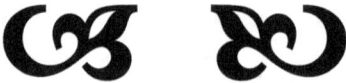

Windows that have been painted, and the paint fused to the glass in a kiln, are another version of **stained glass**.

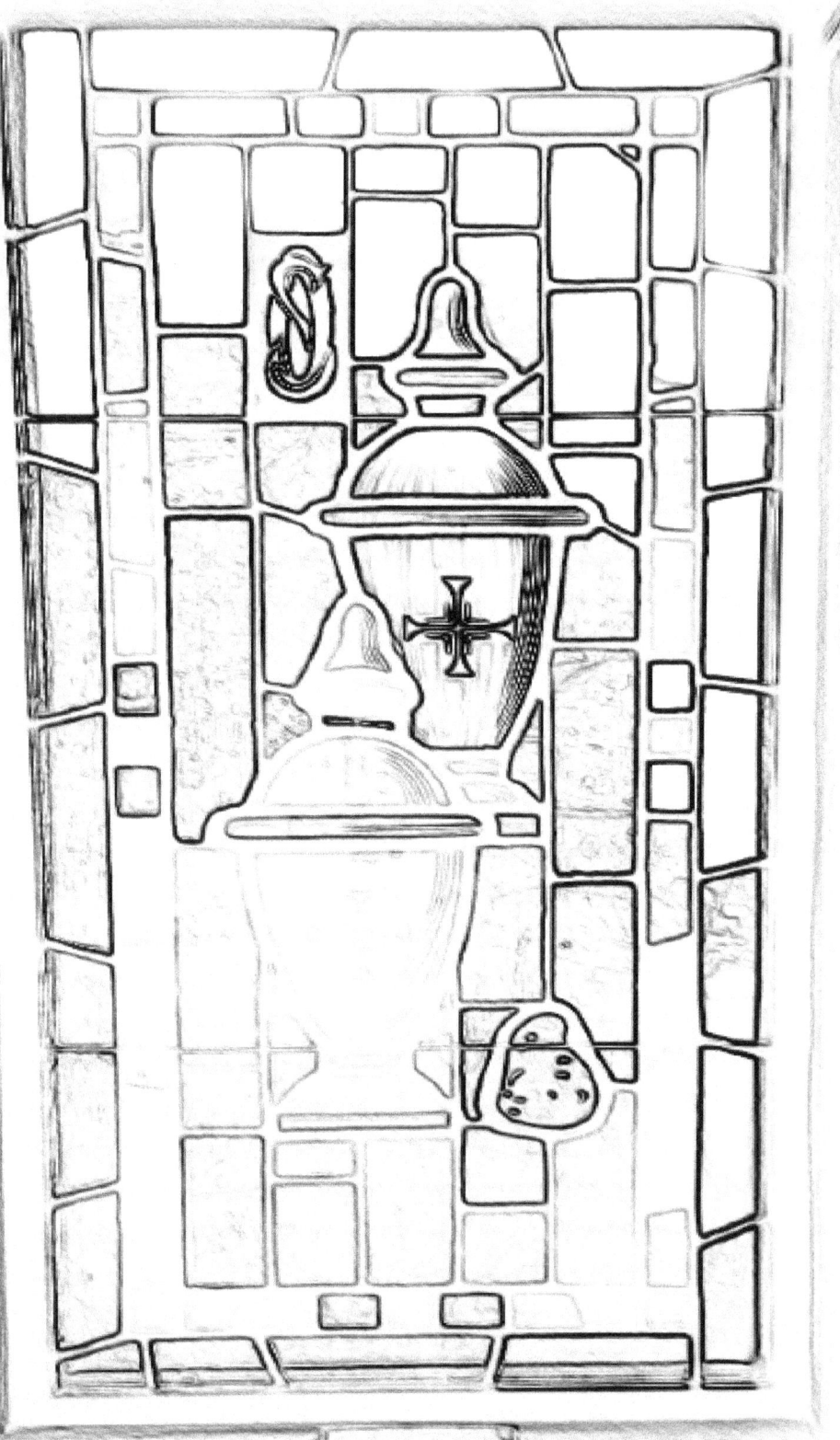

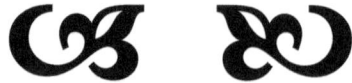

Stained glass windows can be abstract, such as geometric patterns, or symbolic, such as religious or historical stories.

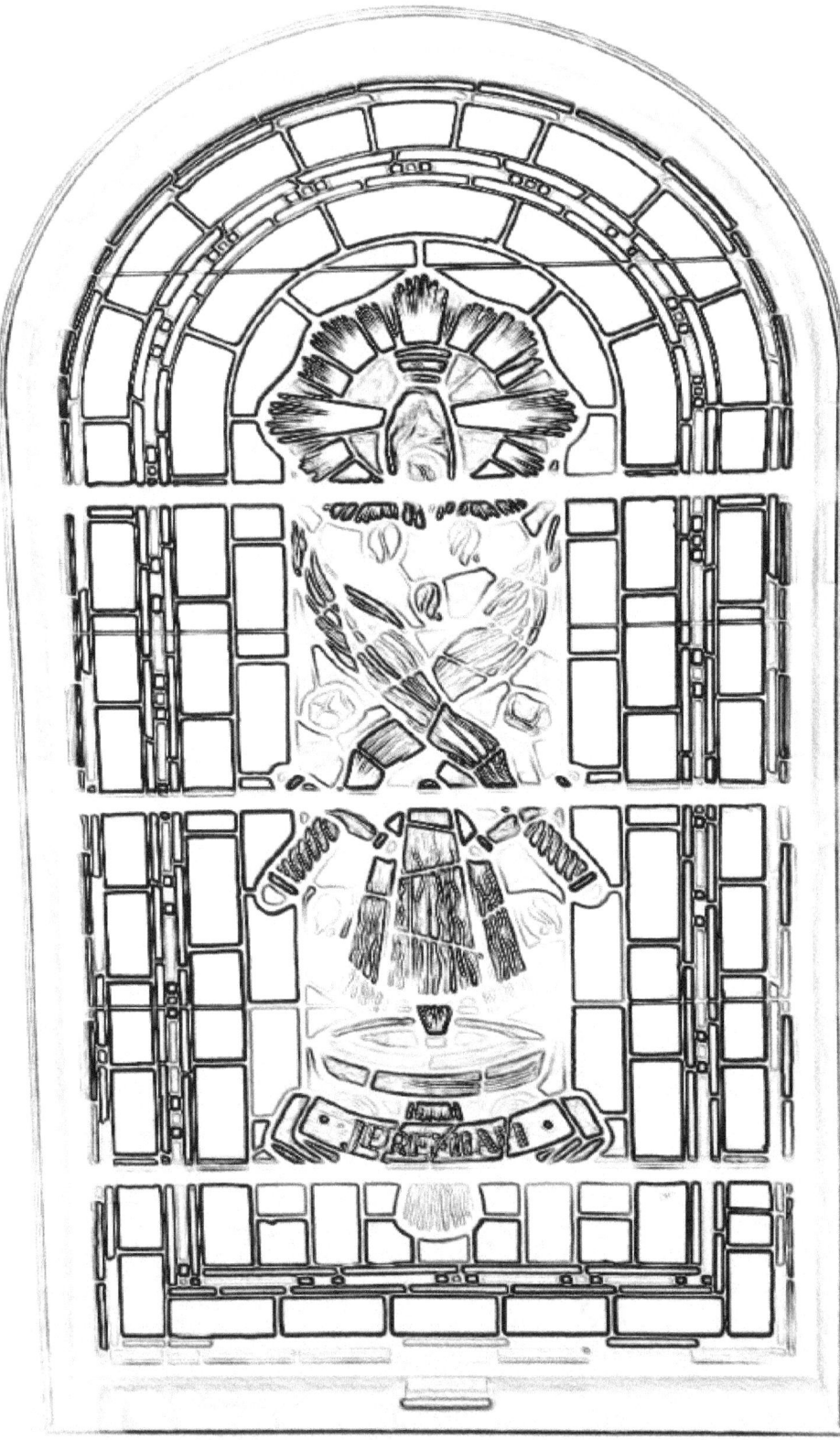

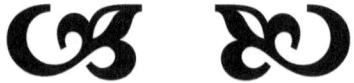

During the Medieval period, glass factories were created near sources of silica, which is an essential element in glass creation.

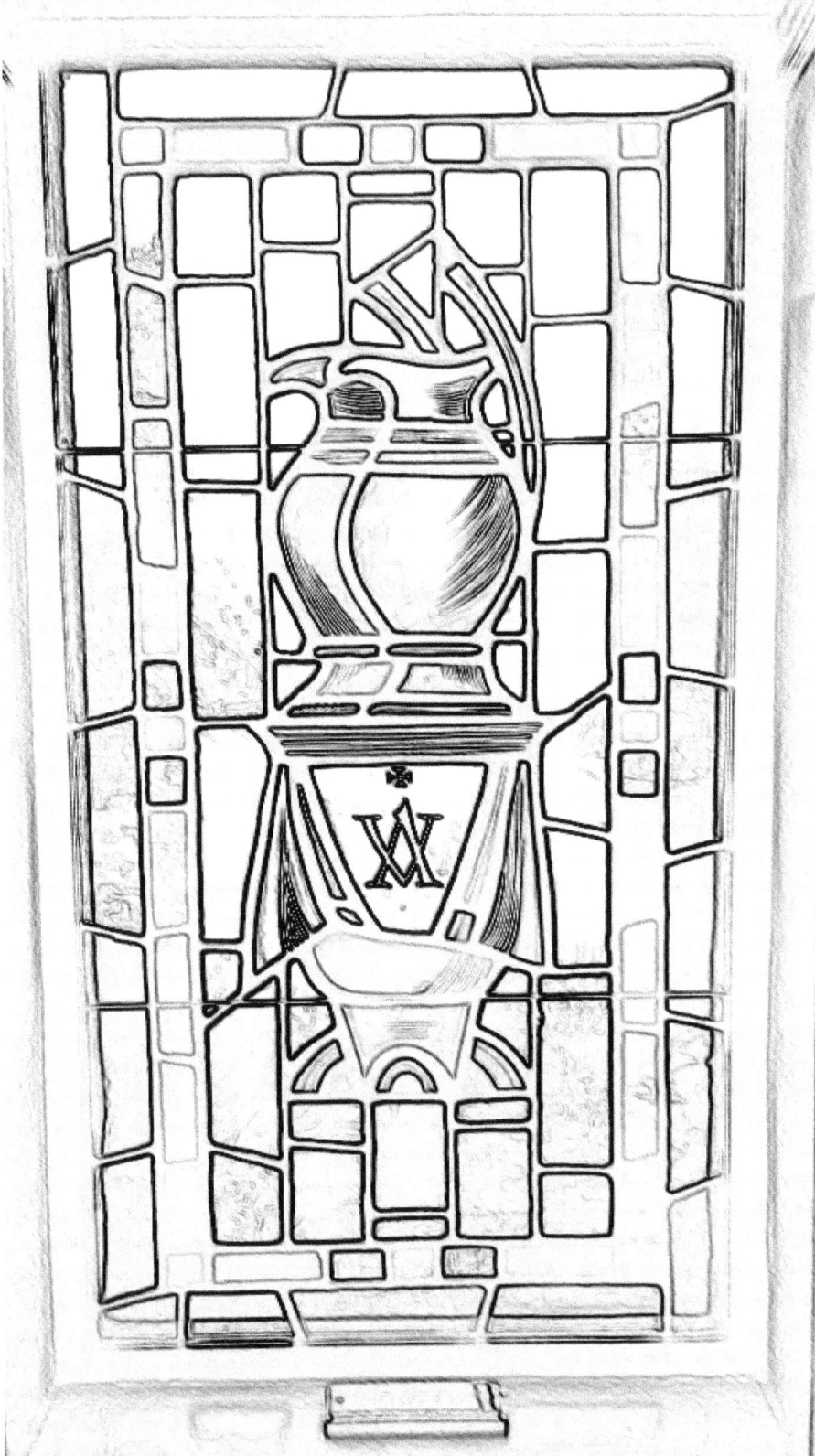

Glass is colored by adding metallic
oxide powders or finely cut metals
when the glass is in a molten state.

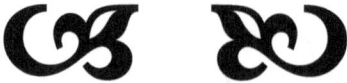

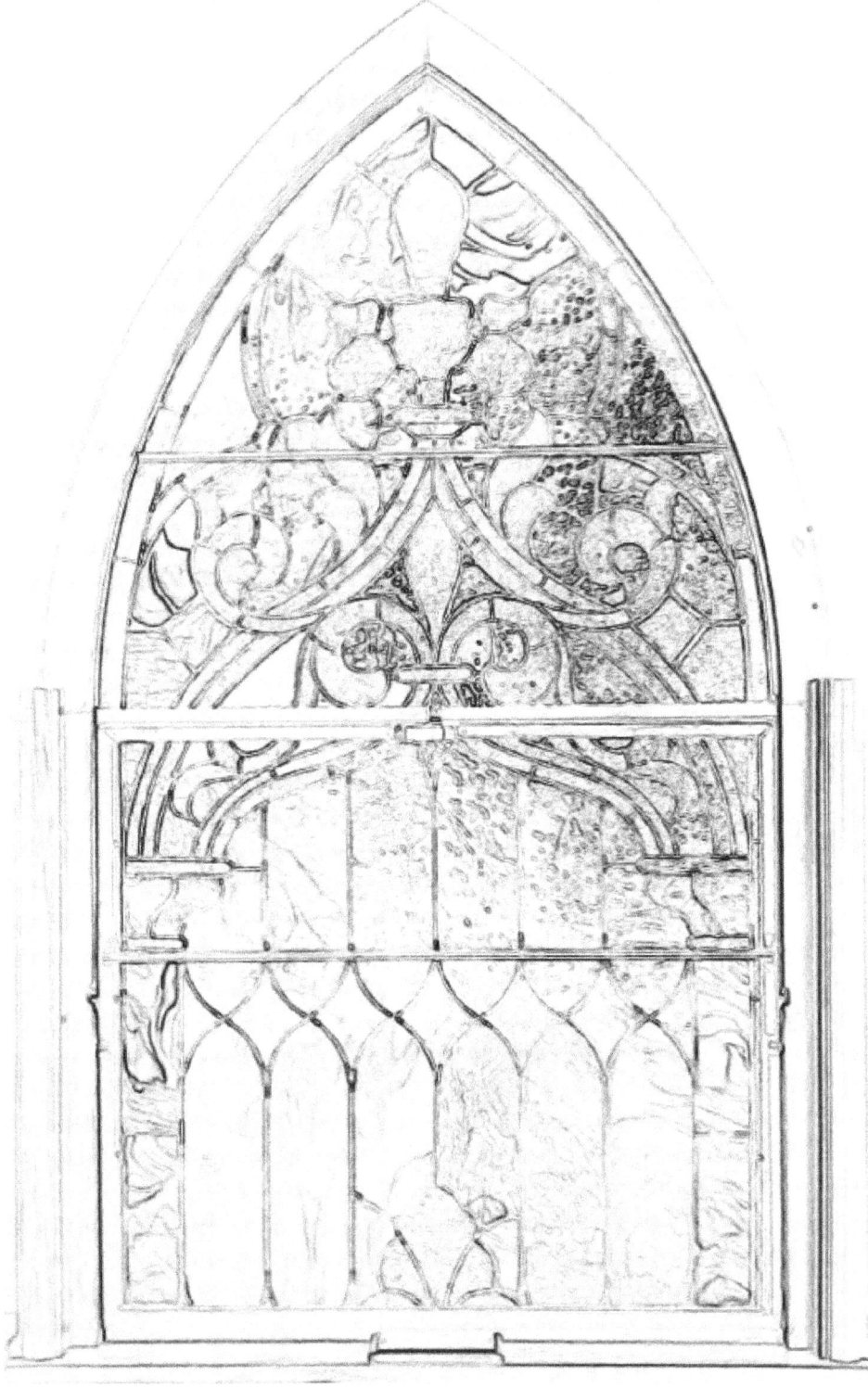

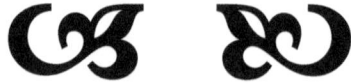

Different materials create different colors when added to molten glass. Copper oxides produce green shades, cobalt makes a deep blue, copper produces a red glass, and gold produces a wine red and violet glass.

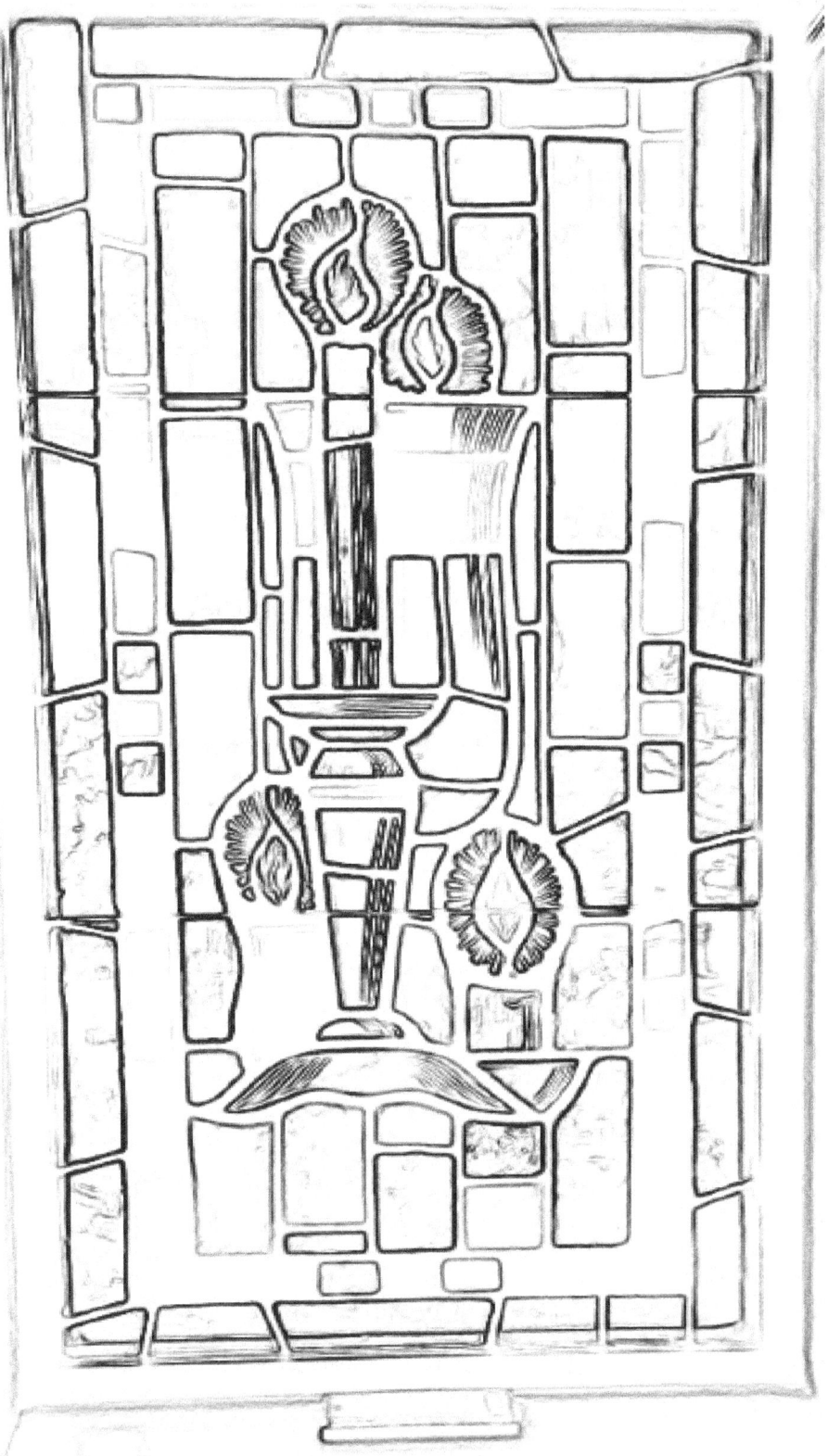

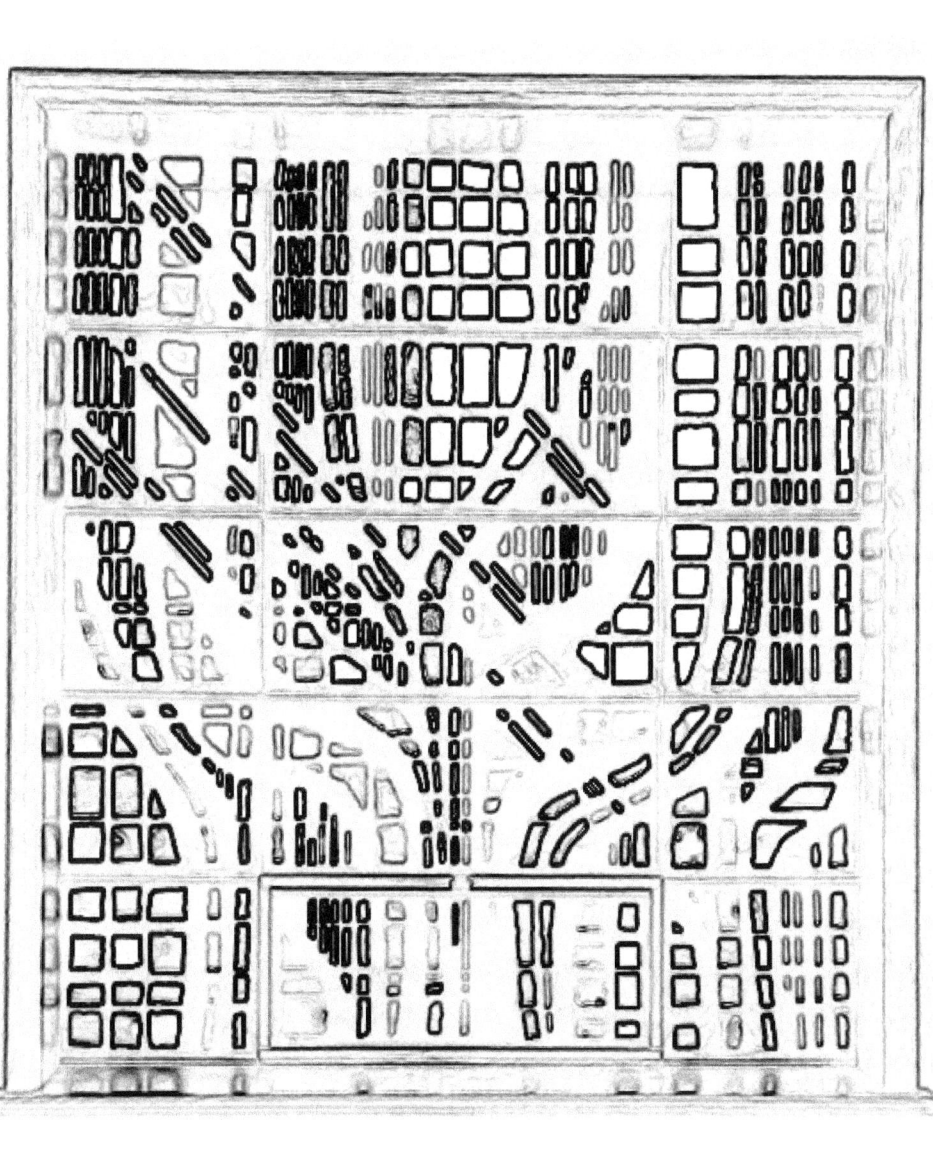

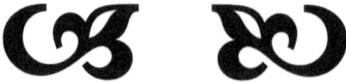

To begin in making a **stained glass** window, precise measurements of the window opening must be performed to create a template.

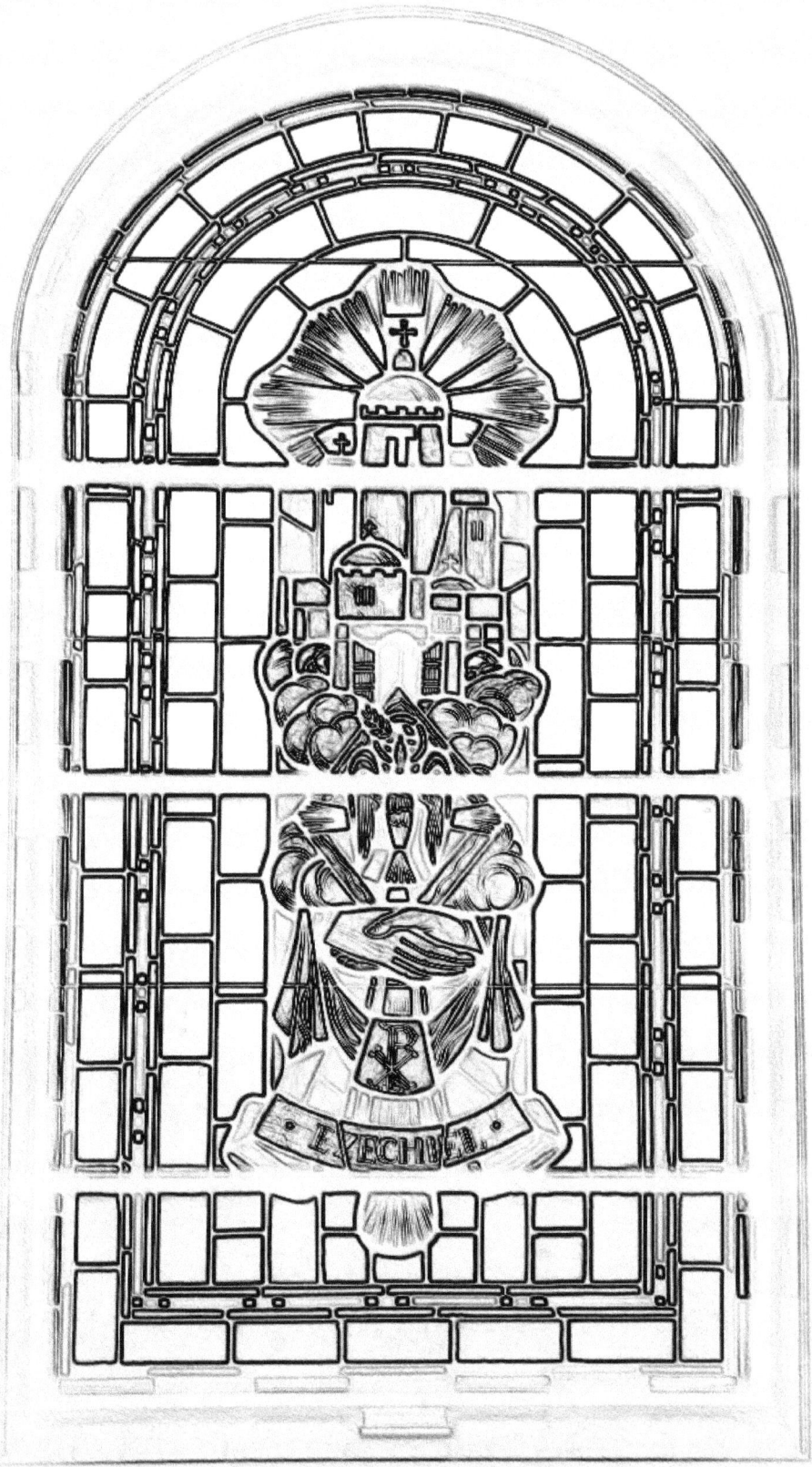

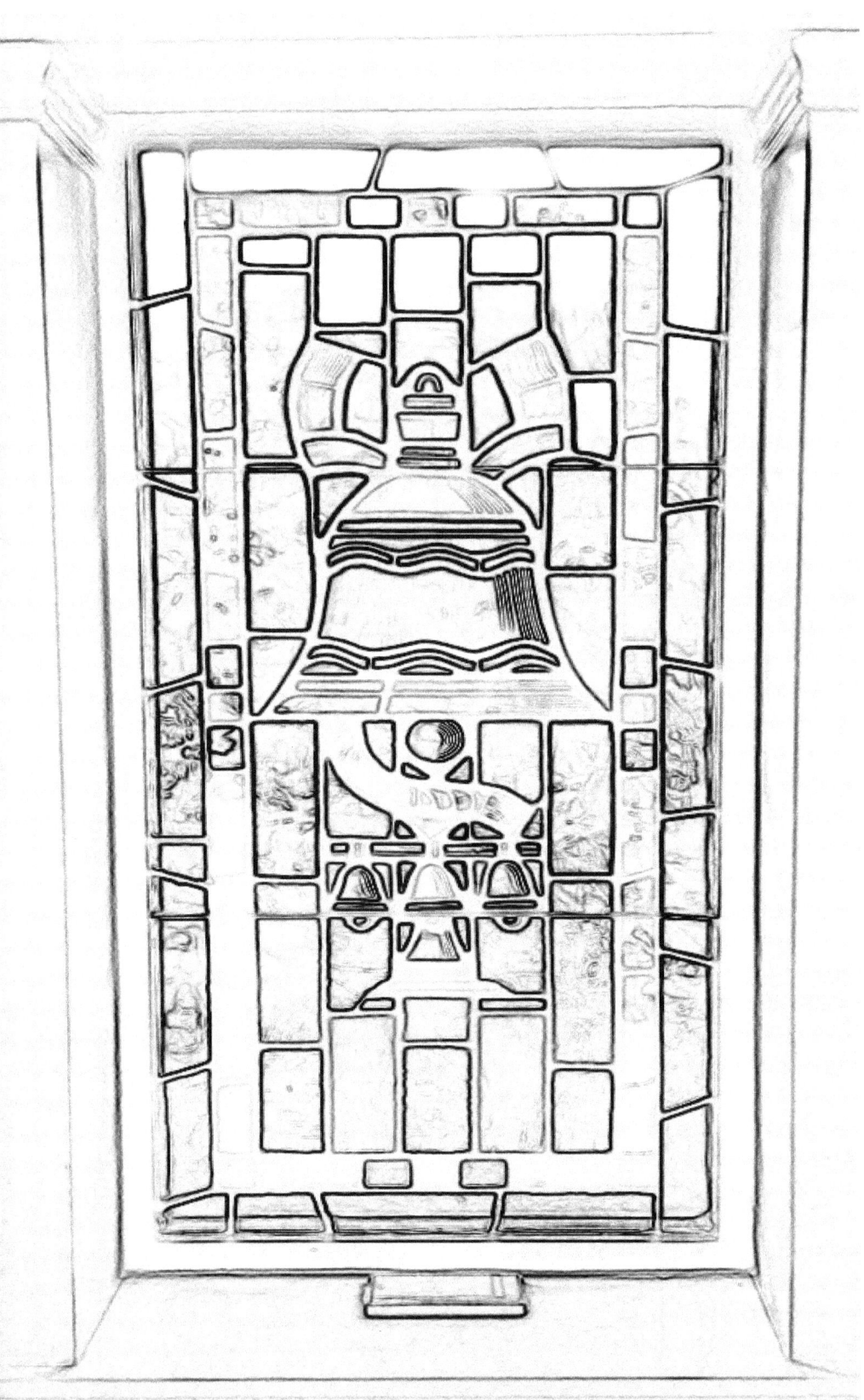

An accurate size drawing must be created for each opening of the window. This drawing is then divided into smaller parts to create templates for glass pieces to be set.

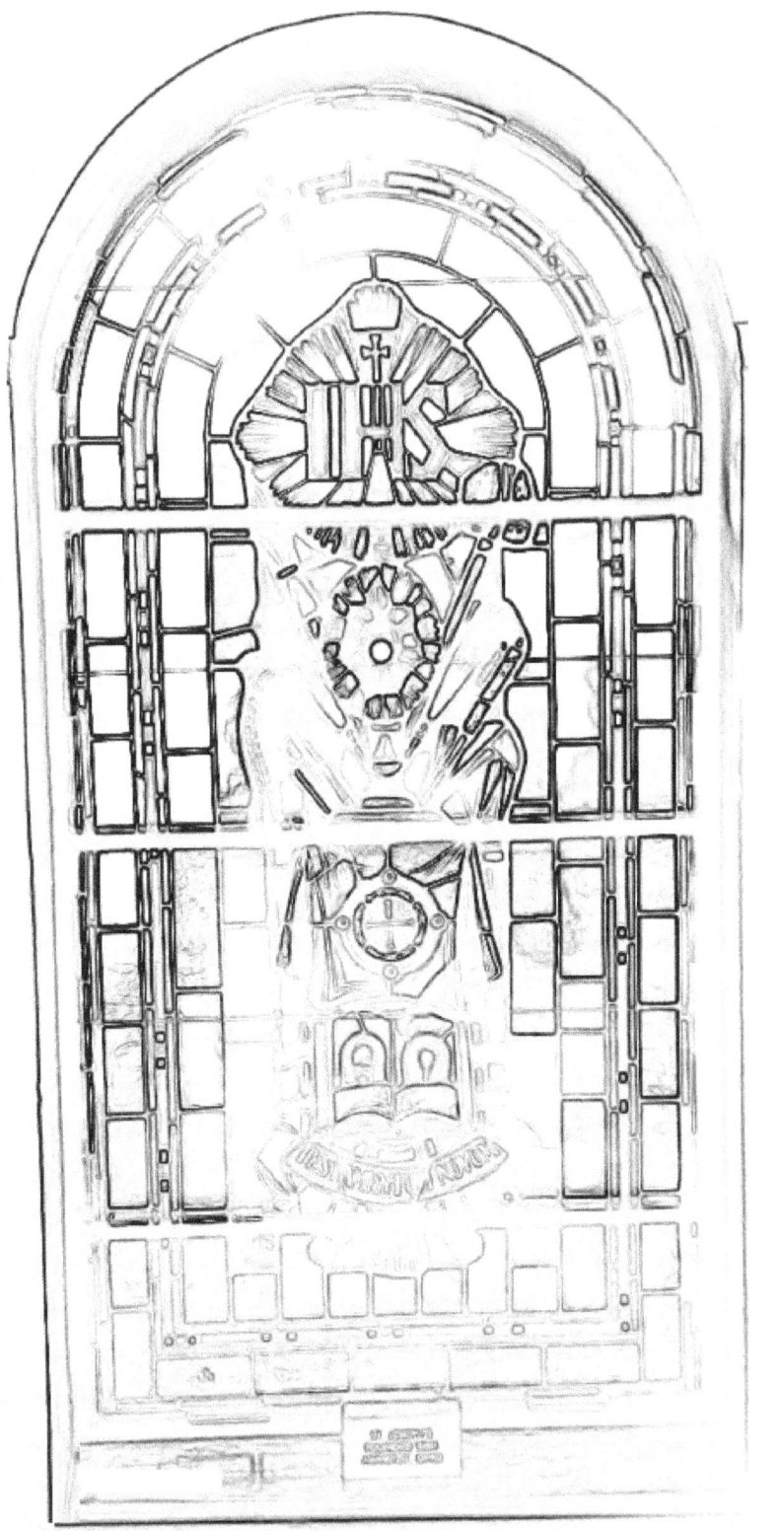

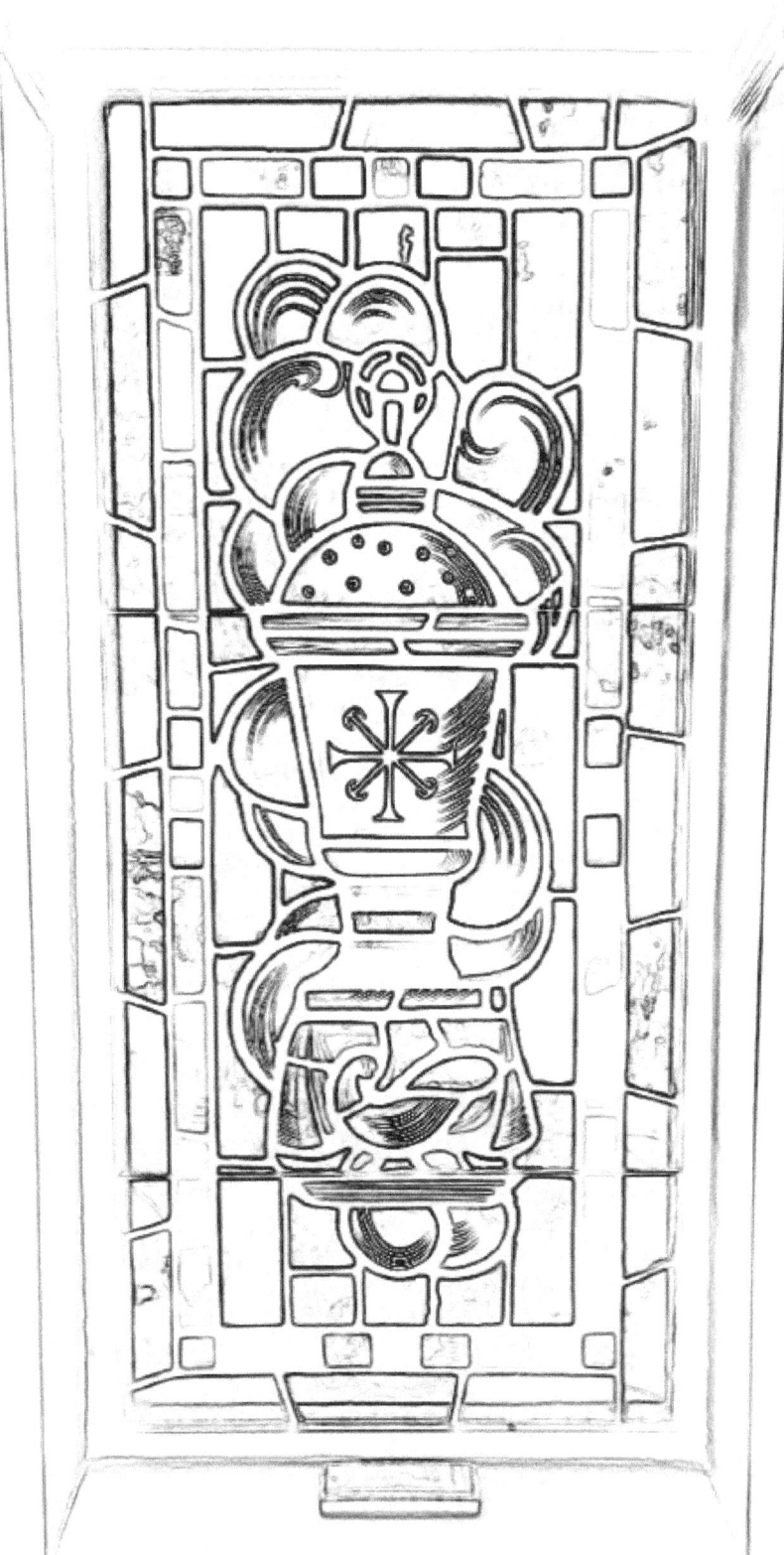

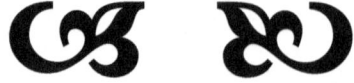

Every piece of glass is carefully chosen, based on its size and color, before it can be arranged in the template.

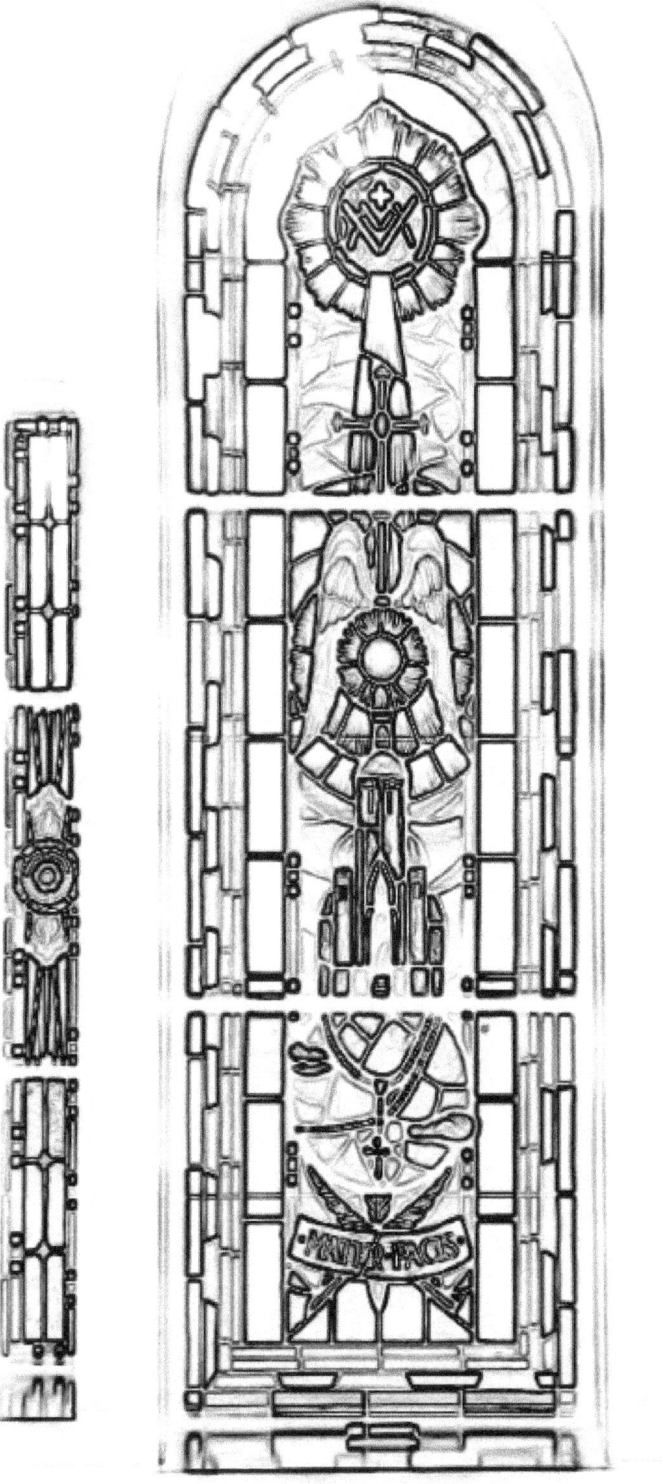

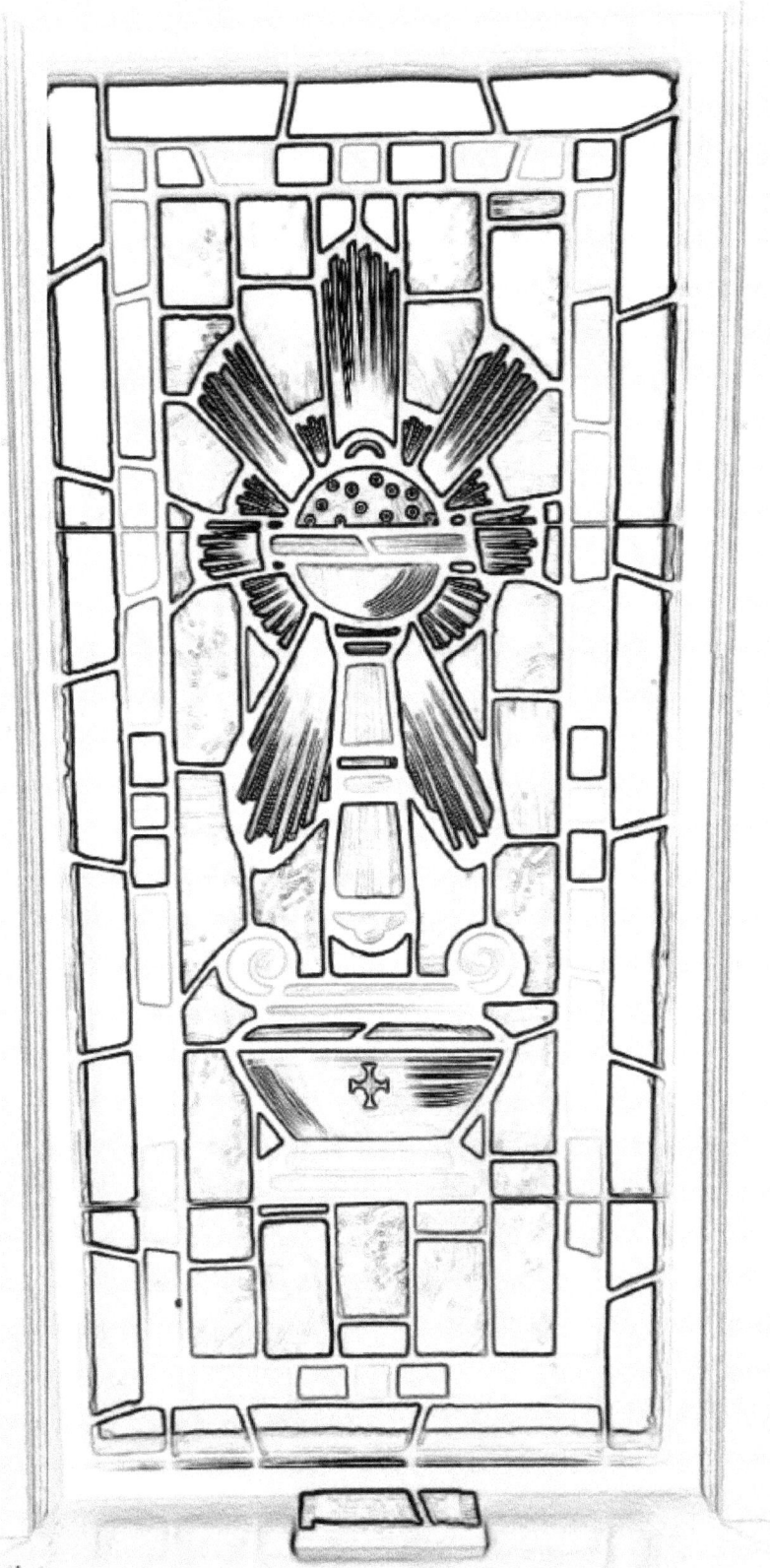

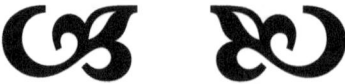

Grozing is the act of cutting small bits of glass from the edges to ensure the entire piece can properly fit in the desired location.

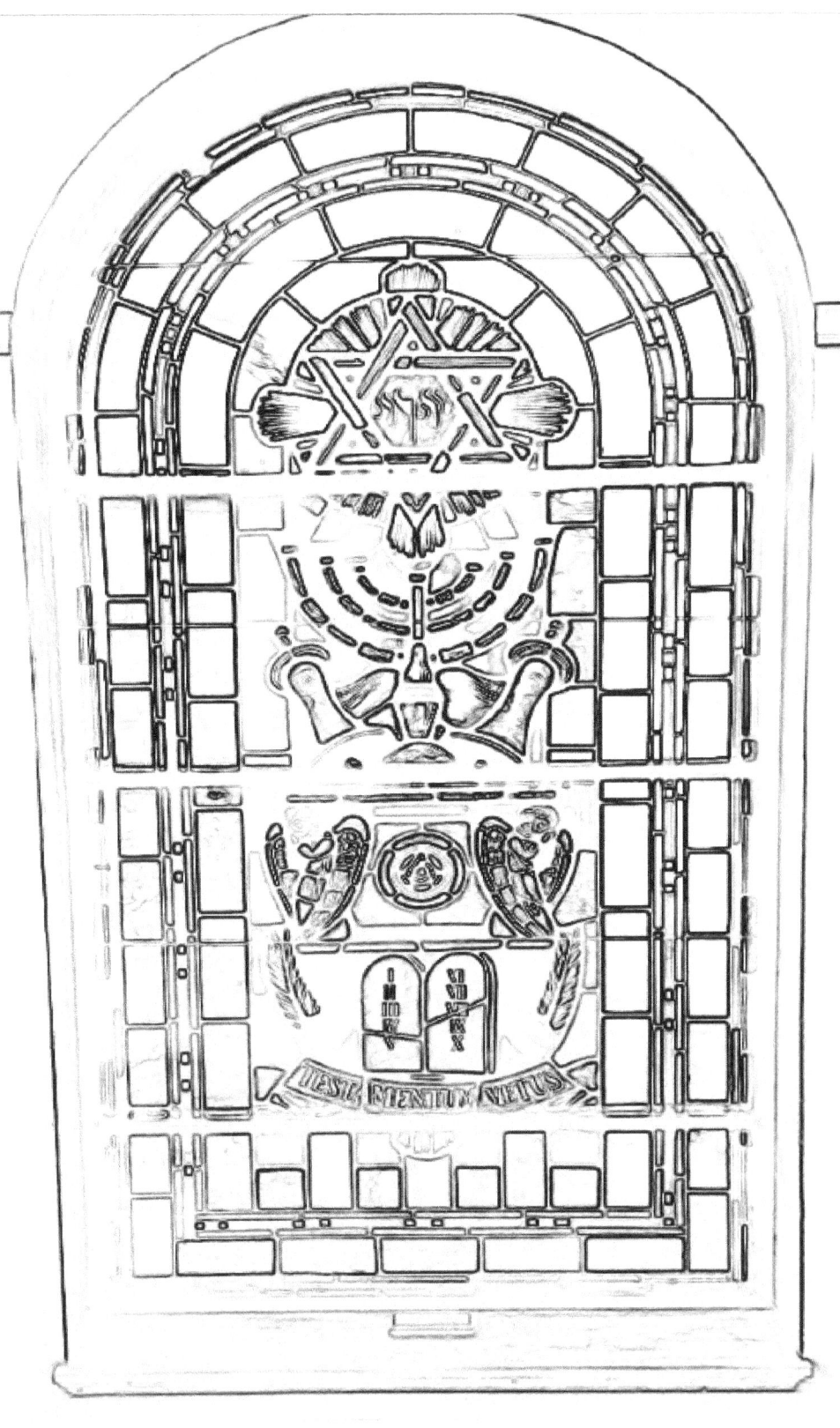

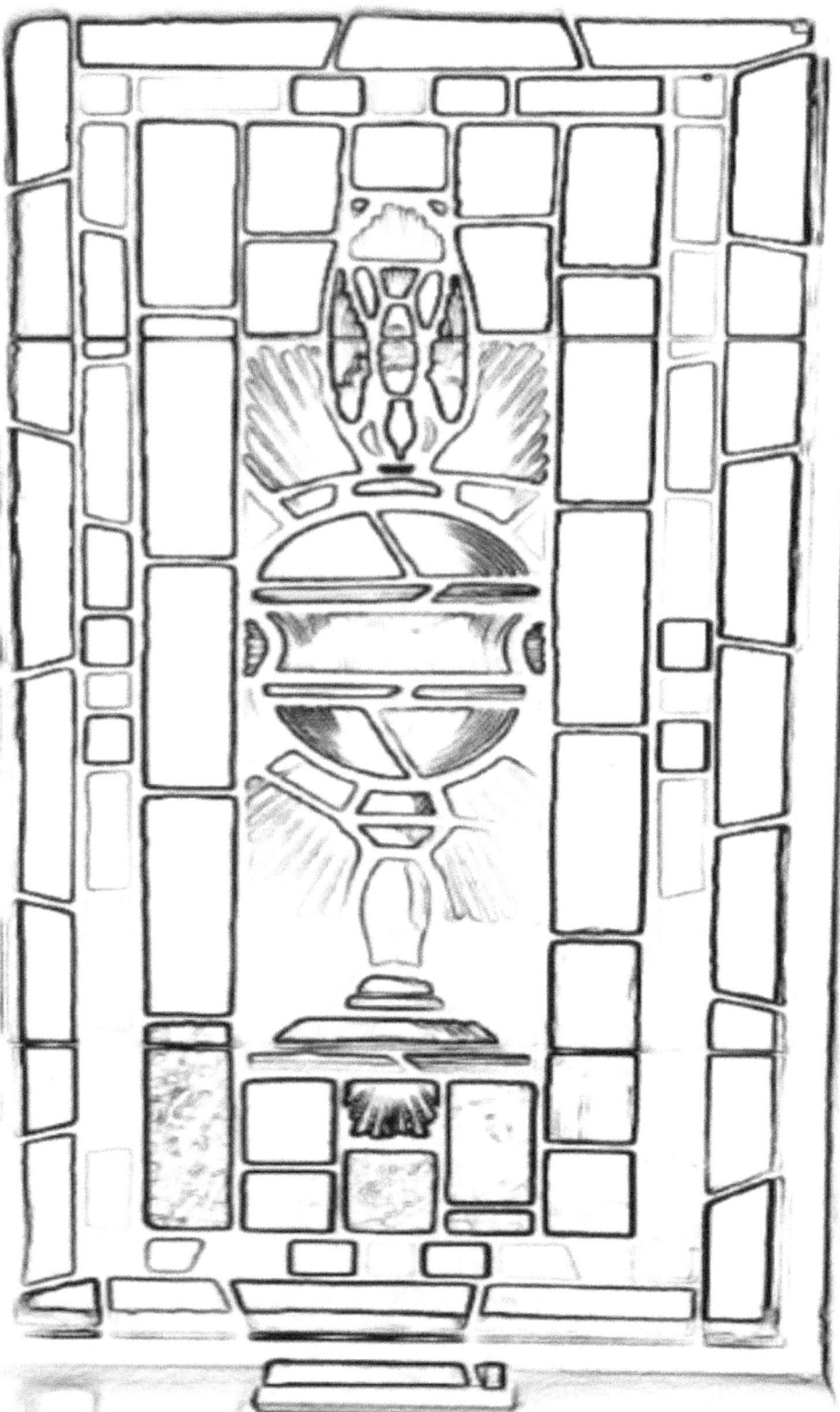

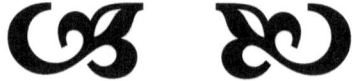

Fine artistic details, such as hair or eyes, can be painted onto the inner surface of the glass using unique glass paint. This paint is created using powdered metals, stones, and glass.

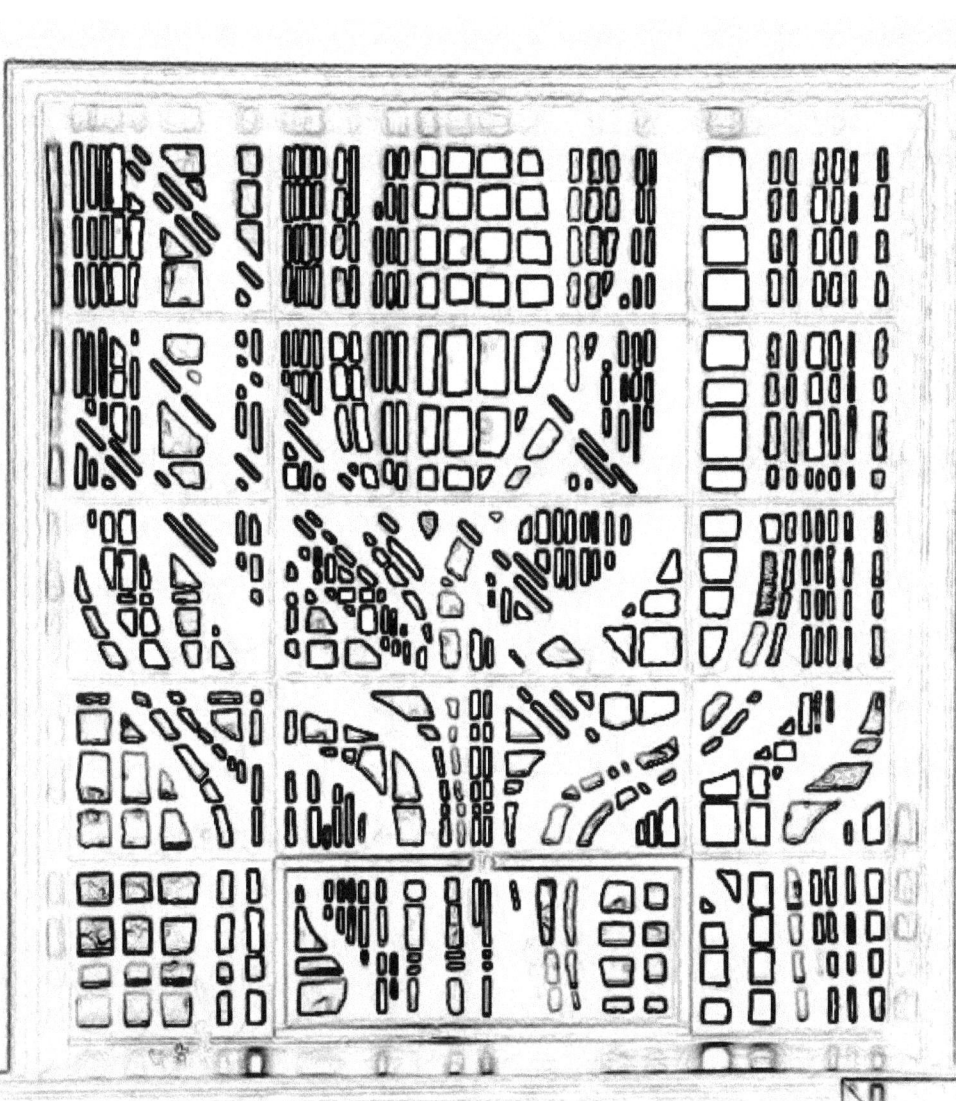

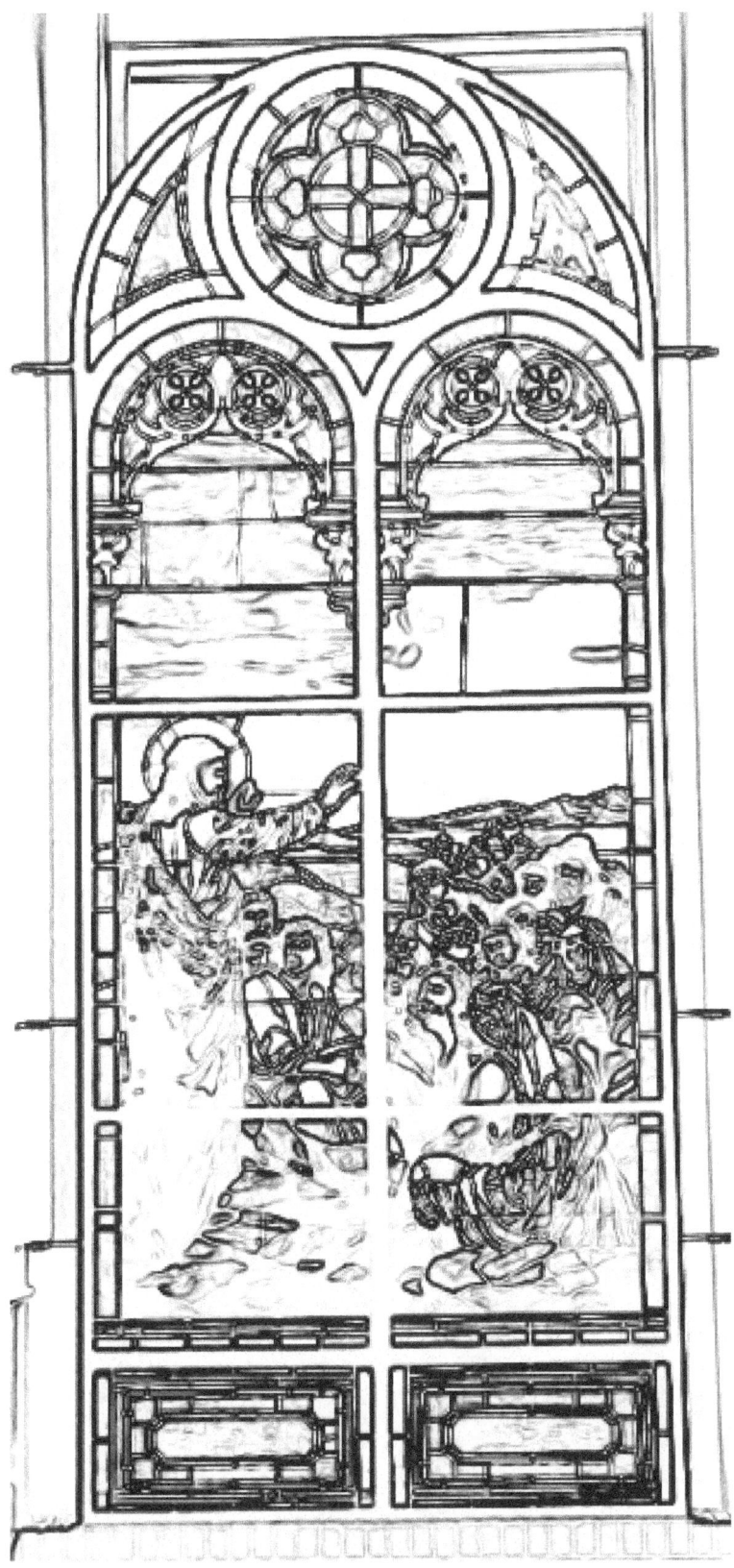

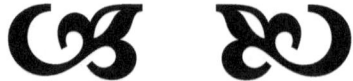

After all the pieces of glass are created, cut, and painted they are set into the frame using a soft metal called lead came.

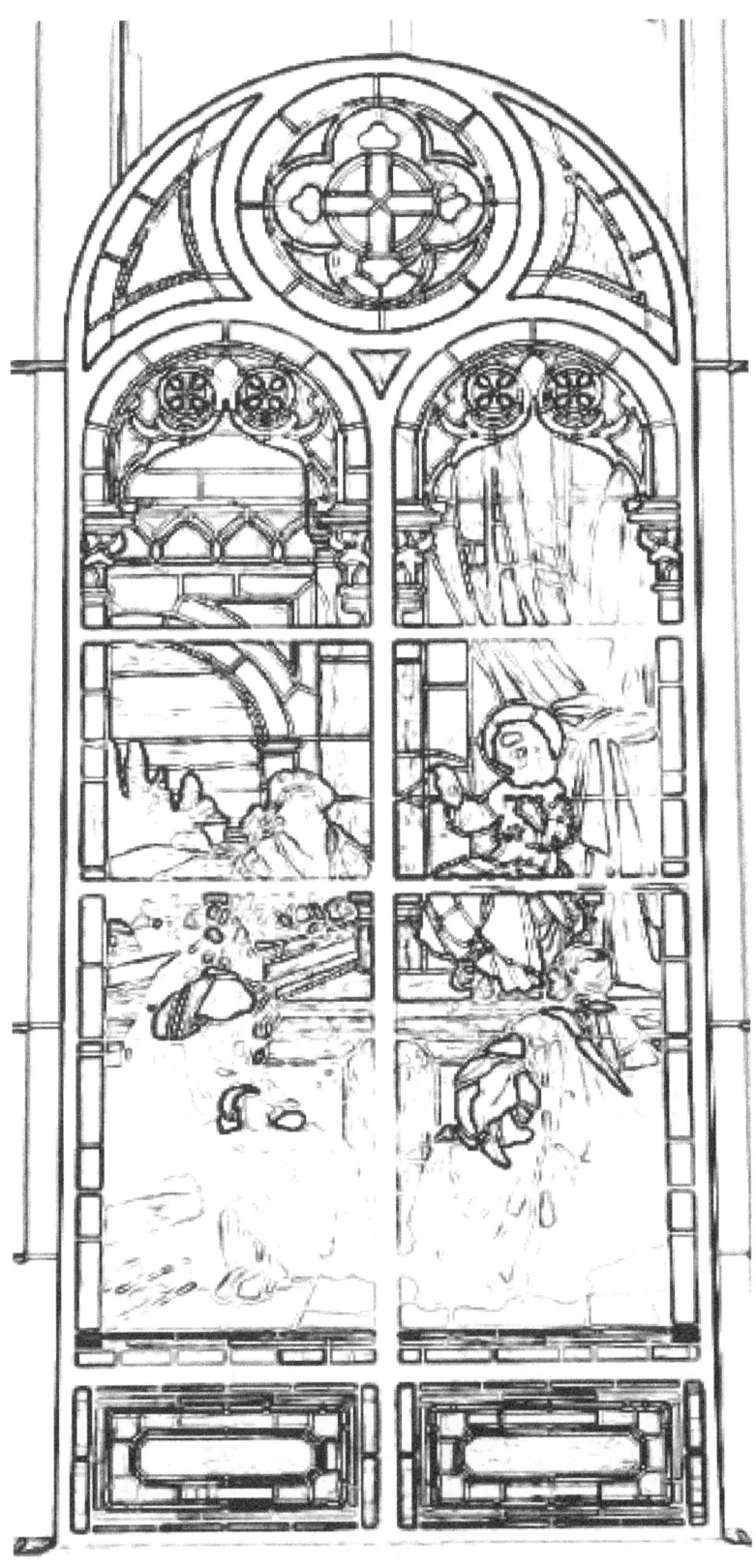

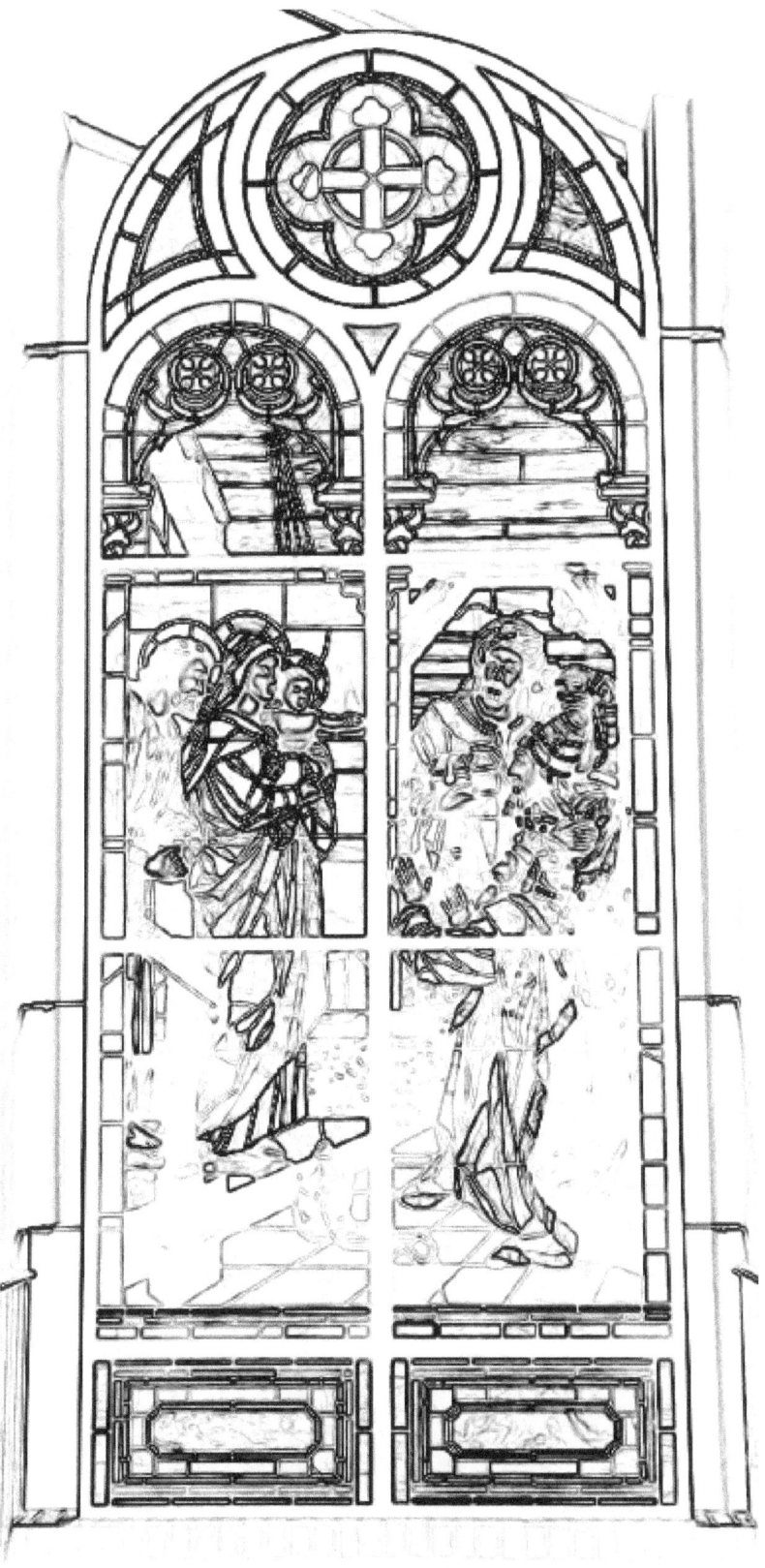

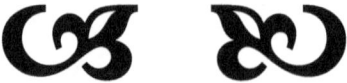

To prevent the glass pieces in a **stained glass** window from moving, they are soldered together. The item is then weatherproofed to protect it from the elements.

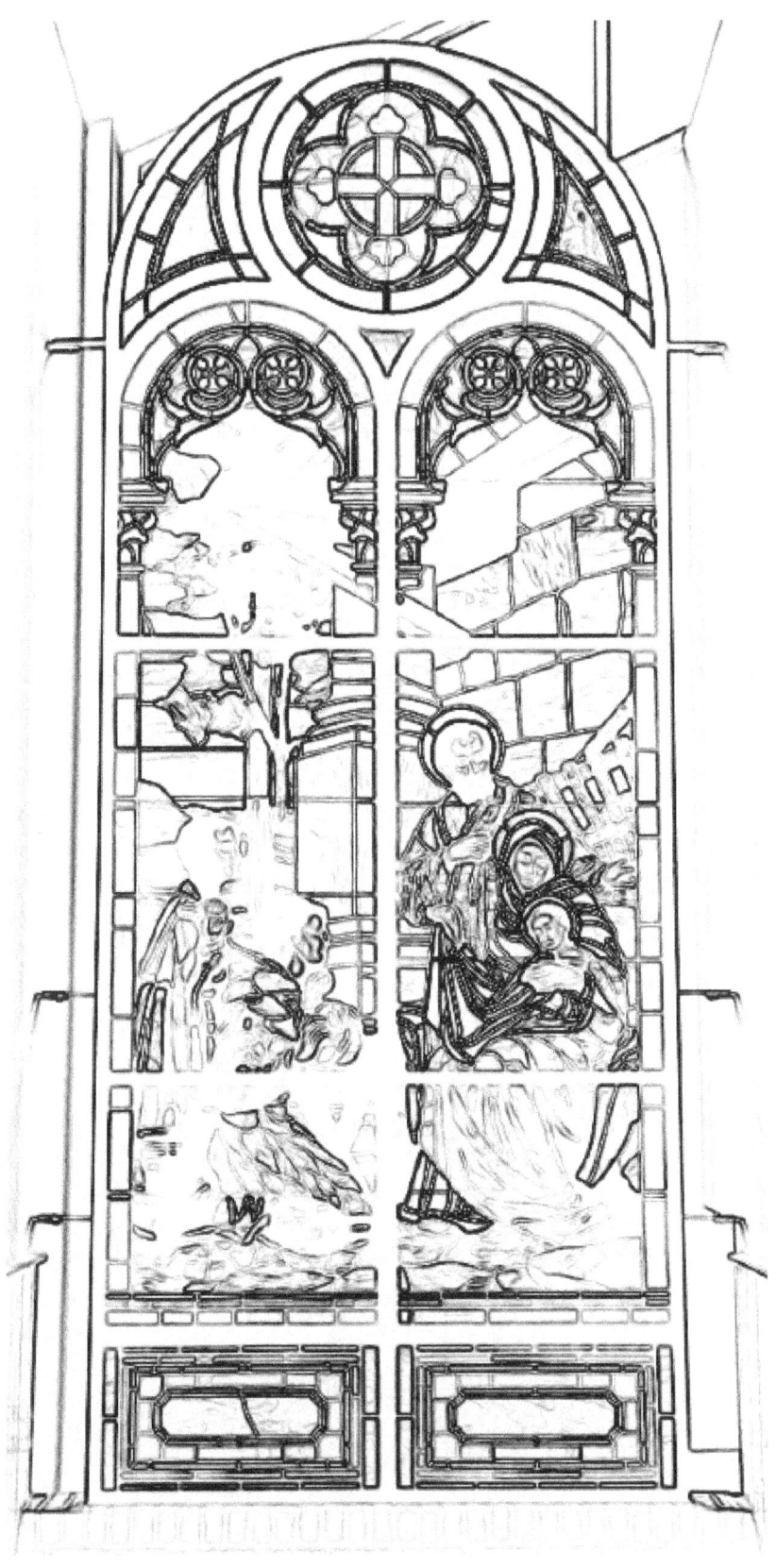

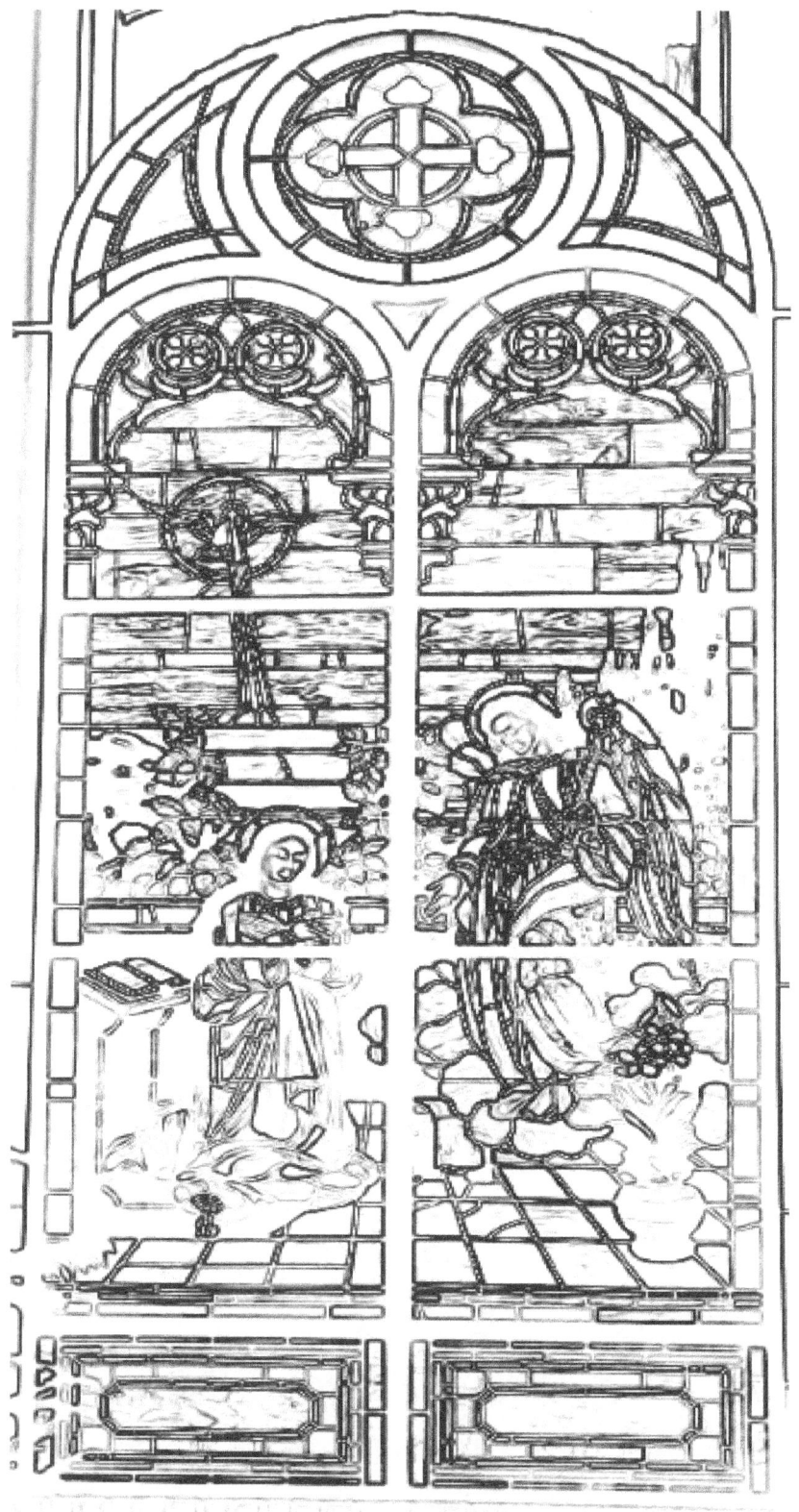

Originally, iron rods were placed across **stained glass** windows at varying points to support the weight of these heavy pieces.

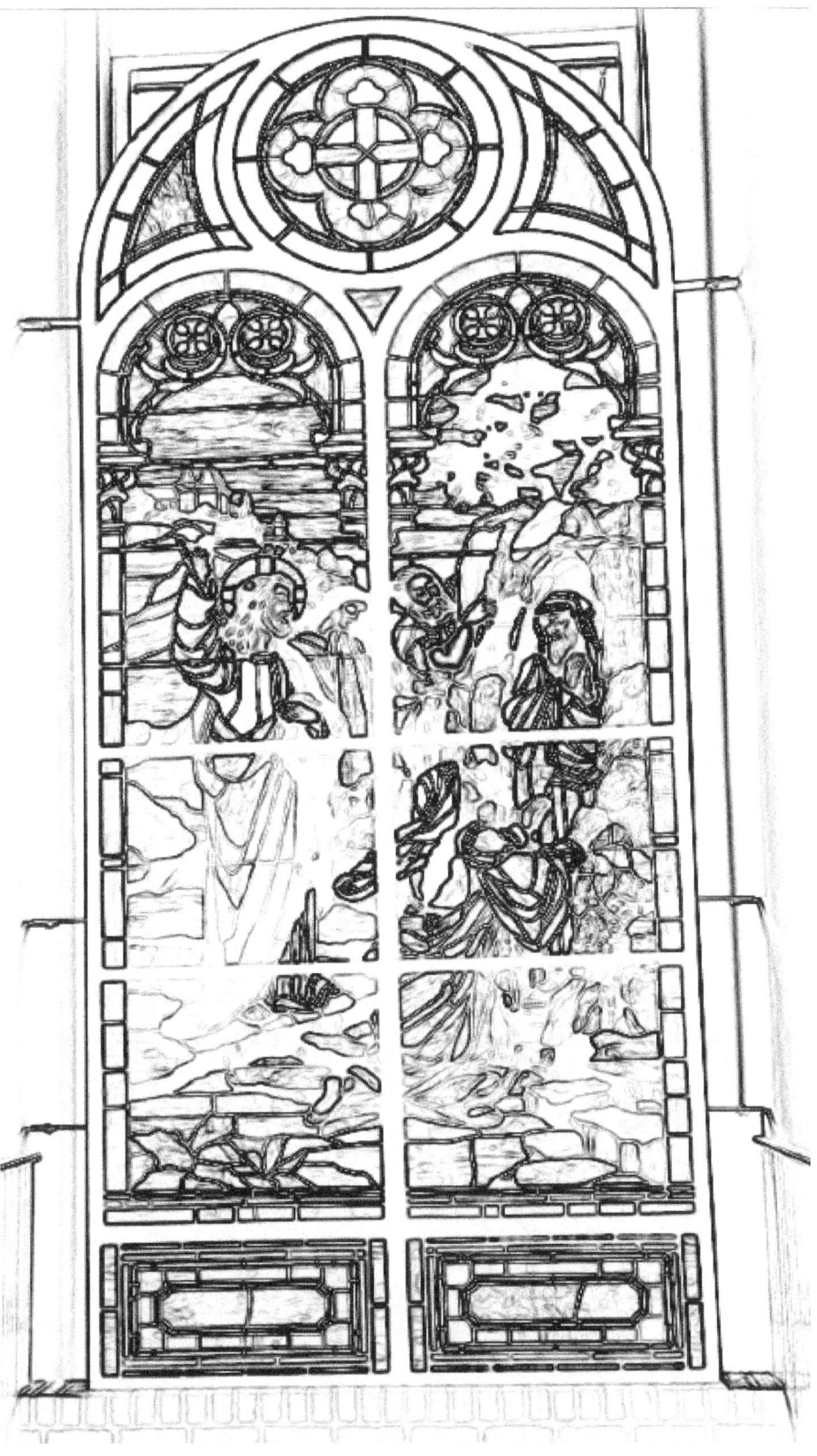

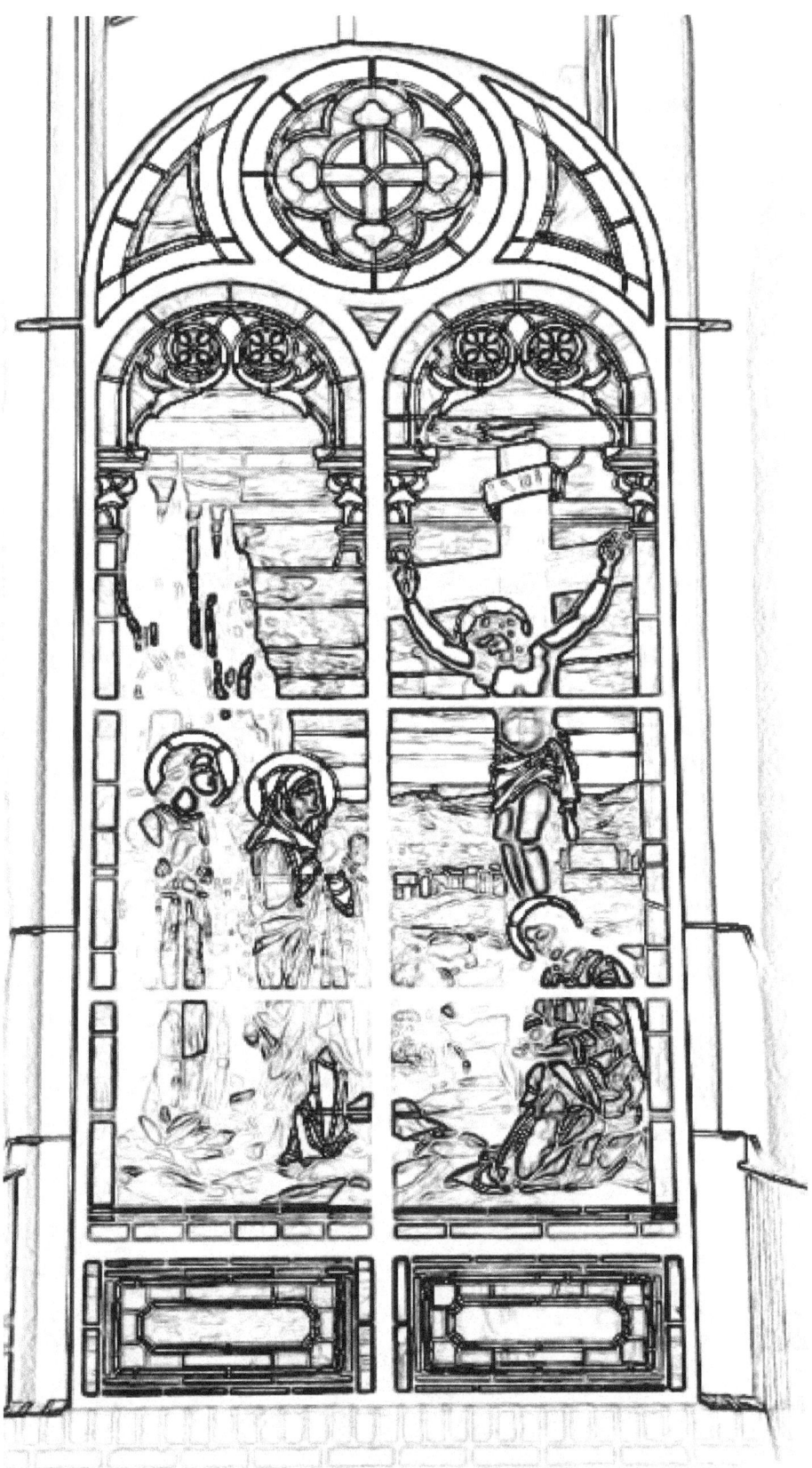

❧ ❧

Colored glass has been produced since ancient times. The Romans and Egyptians were excellent producers of small colored glass objects.

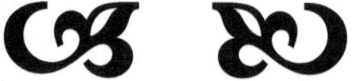

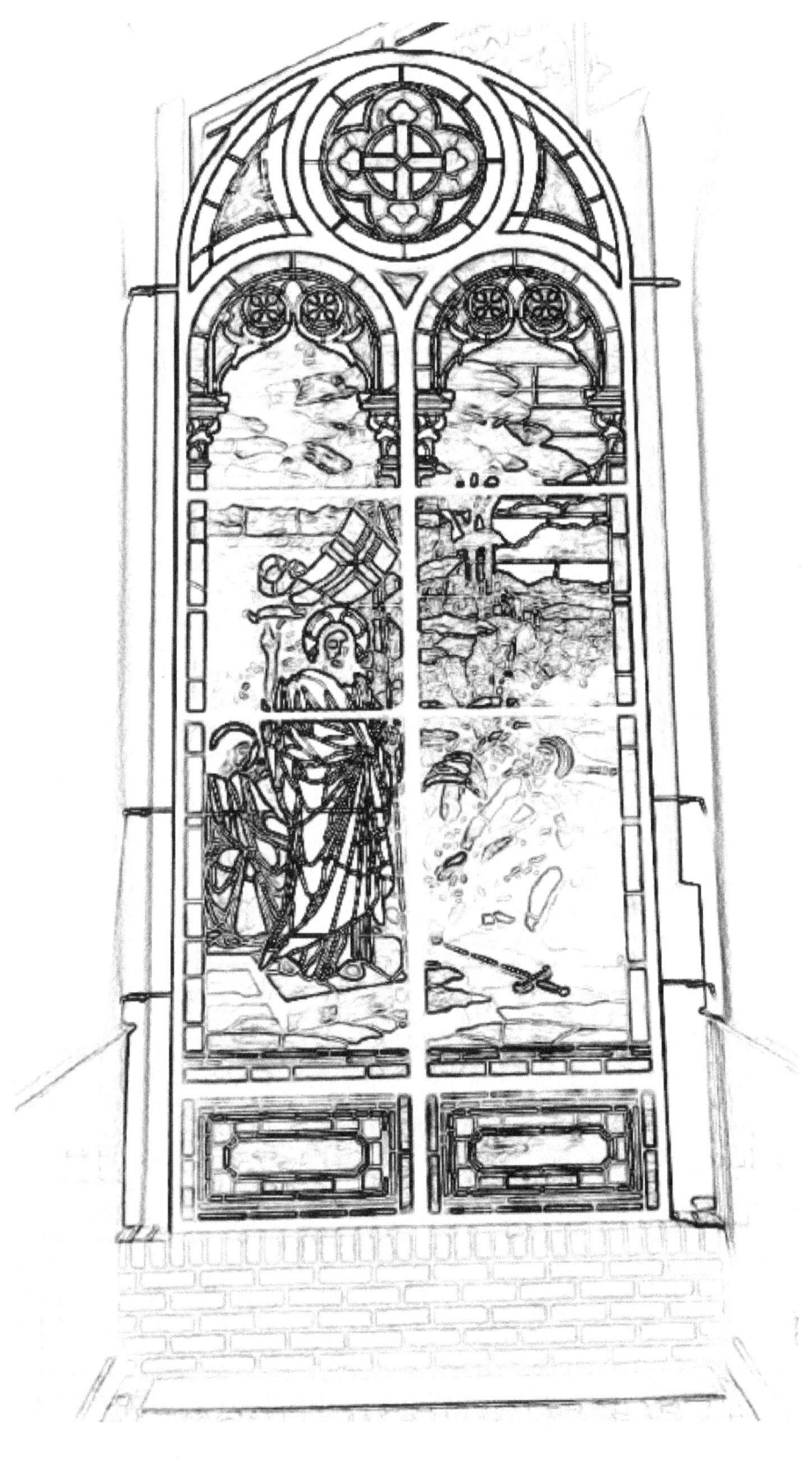

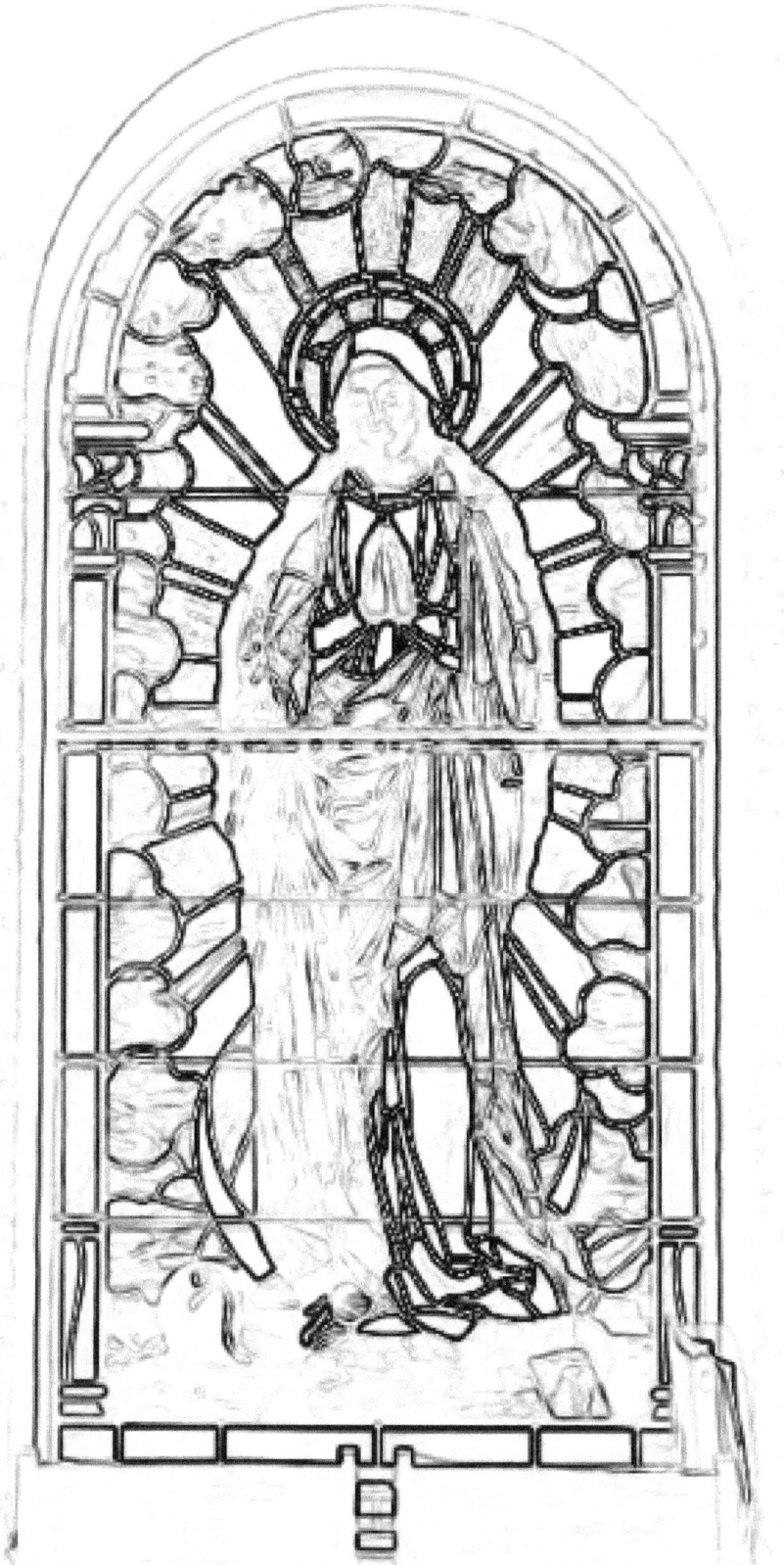

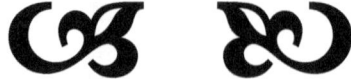

Stained glass windows can be found in British churches and monasteries as early as the 7th century.

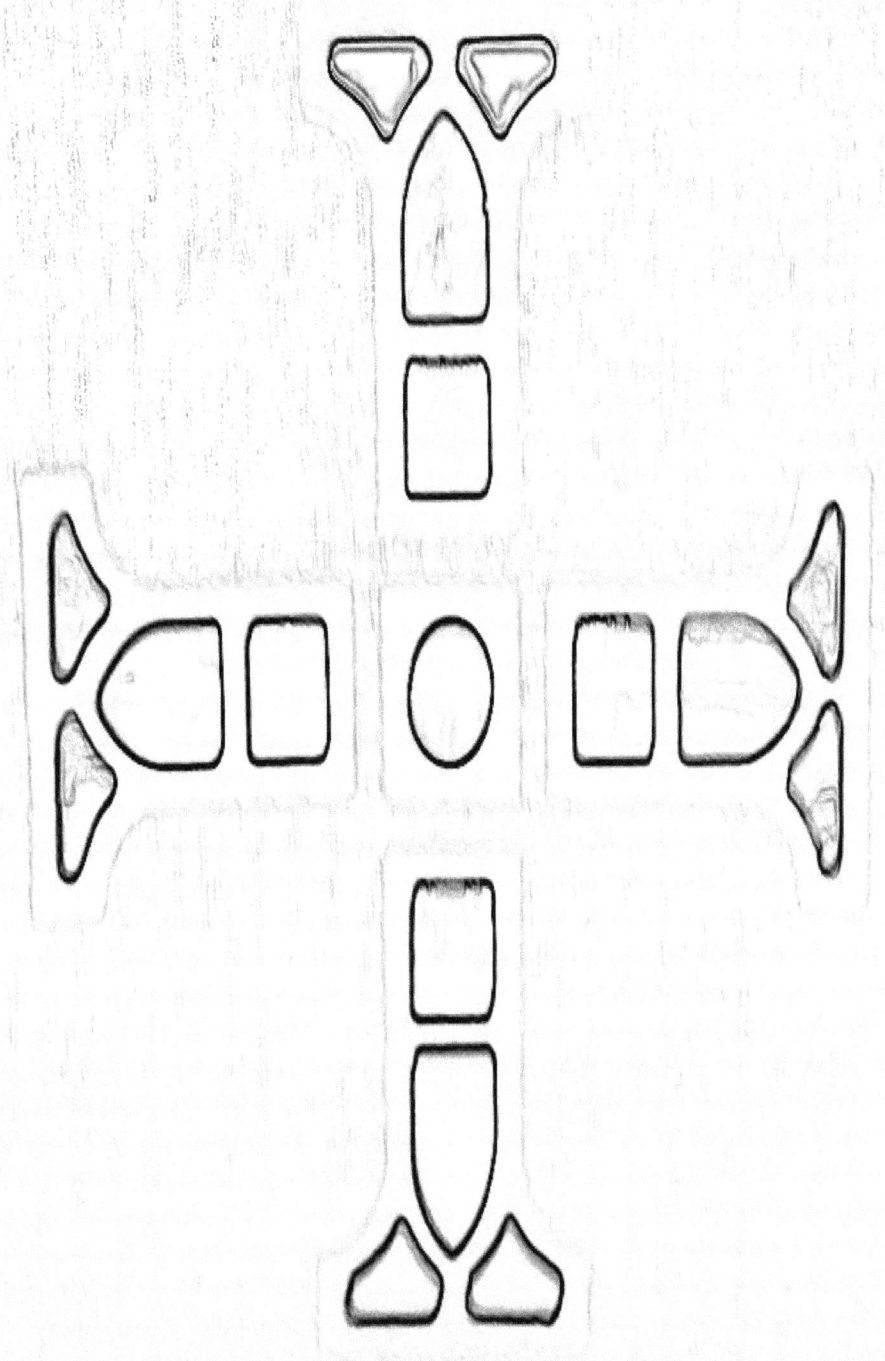

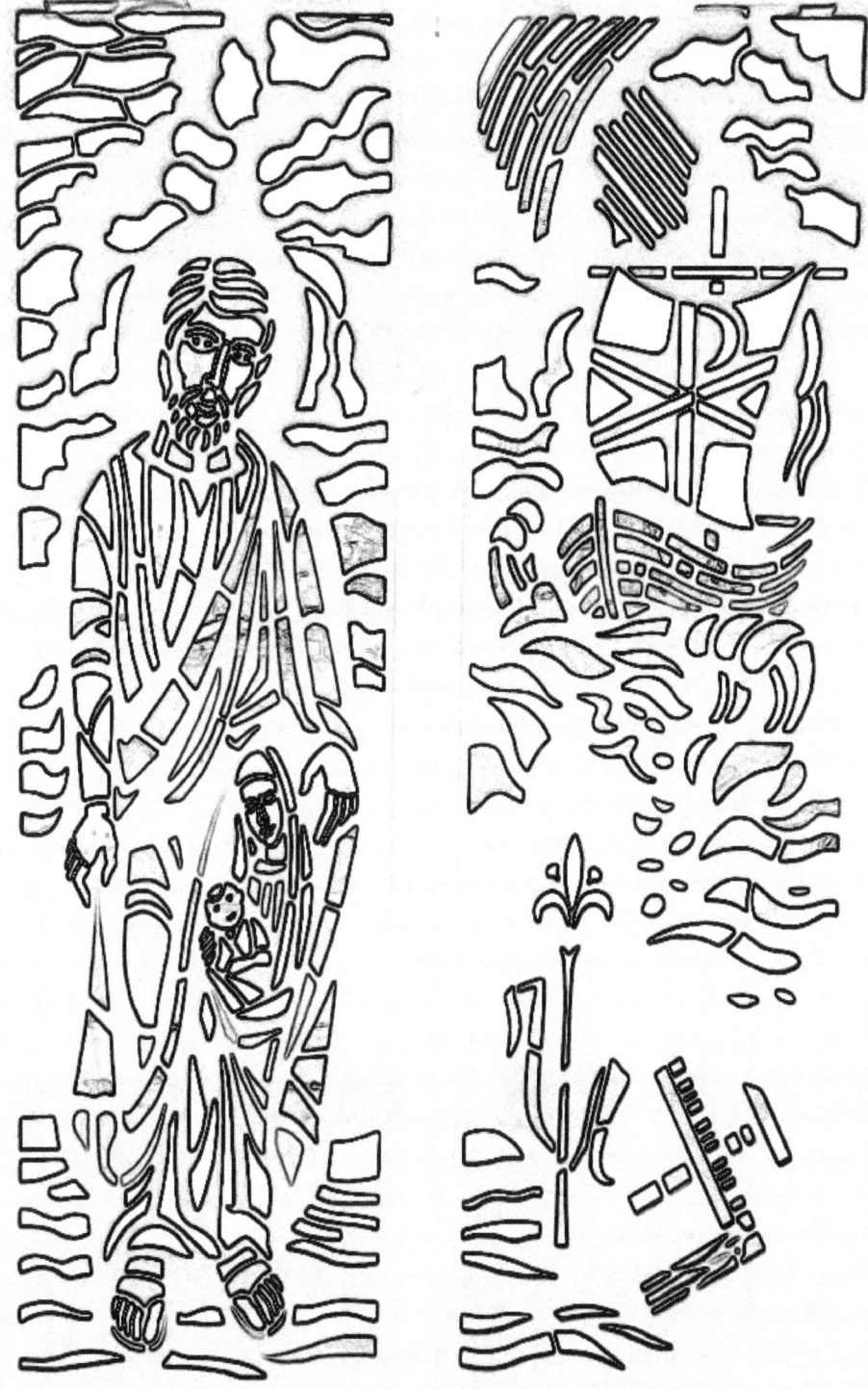

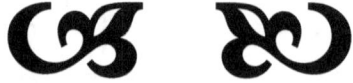

In the Middle Ages, **stained glass** was widely used to educate the masses on stories from the Bible.

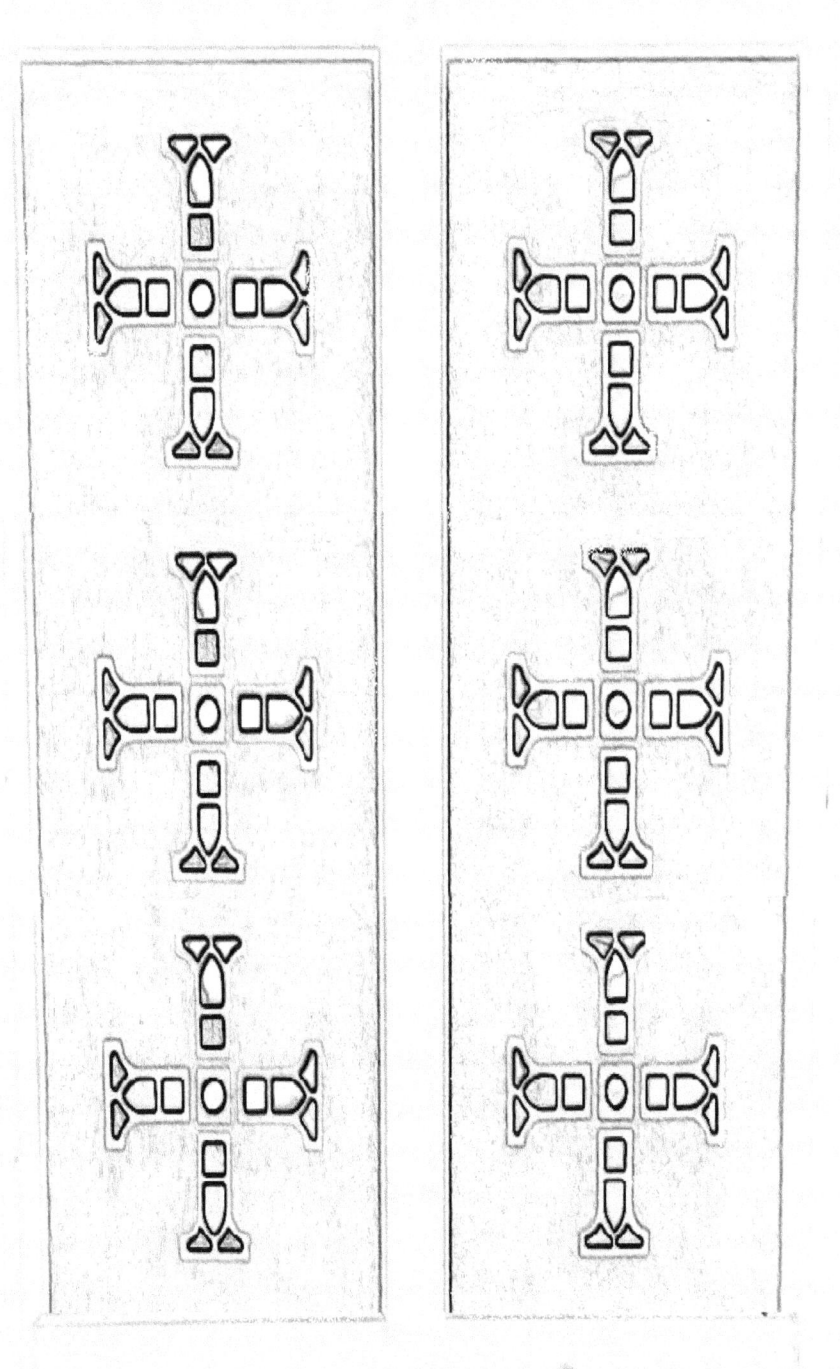

I hope you enjoyed this
Stained Glass Coloring Book.

Post your colored pages to the
Stained Glass Coloring Book Facebook fan page.
@ **http://bit.ly/StainedGlassColoringBook**
& Facebook.com/Stained-Glass-Coloring-Book-559200367576458

And visit the author's website for other products.
www.AuthorRichardETodd.com